Pretty Isn't the PROBLEM

Why We Chase
Youth and Beauty–

And What Really Matters

SHELLI NETKO

Pretty Isn't the PROBLEM

Why We Chase Youth and Beauty— *And What Really Matters*

SHELLI NETKO

heart to heart
PUBLISHING

Pretty Isn't the Problem

Published by Heart to Heart Collective
Scottsdale, Arizona

ISBN: 979-8-9938326-7-8

Printed in the United States of America

Book Layout Design: Abu Bakar Javed

For more resources, visit: shellinetko.com

Dedication

To all the women who spent years searching for their worth in the mirror— May you finally discover it was never there.

And to Ava—
May you always carry the honest view of beauty you had at eight years old.

Beautiful means people who feel good about themselves and are kind to other people.

No performance.
No awareness of being watched.
No pressure to be anything other than who they are.

Because beauty is only skin deep.

Table of contents

PROLOGUE

Where Does It End?

Every woman remembers a moment with a mirror. I know where mine began. It started with a girl standing on a chair in front of the bathroom mirror. She tilted her head from side to side, studying her reflection the way children do – curious, imaginative, wondering what she might look like someday.

Mirrors are innocent companions when we're young. They're places for curiosity.
At first, it's simple—faces, expressions, playing around.

Then it becomes a little more.
A new hairstyle.
A touch of makeup.
A different outfit.

We lean closer, trying on different versions of ourselves.

At that age, the mirror feels like a friend.

But somewhere along the way, something changes.

Years pass.
Life happens.
And one day you catch your reflection again – maybe in a store window, or the bathroom mirror while getting ready for the day.

This time you pause. Not because something is wrong. But because something is different.

The face looking back at you is still yours... but it's no longer exactly the one you remember.

There are lines that weren't there before.
Skin that has softened.
Small reminders that time has been moving forward.

For generations, women have cared about beauty.
There's nothing unusual about wanting to look good.

A flattering outfit.
A new hairstyle.
A little mascara.

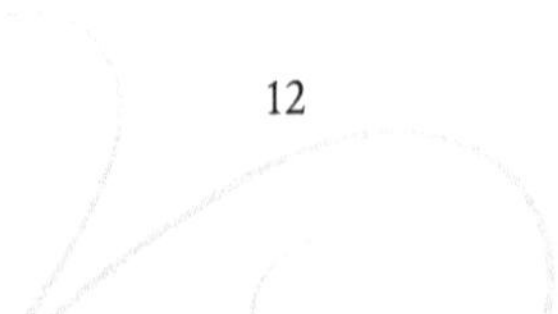

These things can be joyful. Creative. A way of expressing who we are.

But something has shifted.
Looking good used to be enough. Now the expectation often feels like something else entirely. Agelessness. Not twenty at forty. Not forty at sixty. But somewhere in between – suspended in time.

Botox before a wrinkle appears.
Lip injections in your twenties.
Brows lifted.
Lashes extended.
Skin resurfaced.
Jawlines sculpted.

Beauty used to be about enhancing what we were born with. But somewhere along the way, the mirror stopped being just a reflection and became a quiet negotiation with time.

Time keeps moving. The mirror keeps changing.

And some of us never pause to ask the question we might already be thinking but are afraid to say outloud—how far do I want to take this?

For many, it simply becomes routine—scheduled appointments, fillers, Botox, microneedling—whatever it takes, trying to hold on to a version of ourselves that time was never meant to freeze.

My own relationship with beauty began with a belief that settled quietly into my mind when I was young.

I thought I was ugly.
Average at best.

That belief shaped how I saw myself for years. It influenced how I experimented with beauty, how I responded to attention, and how much meaning I placed on what the mirror showed me.

Like many women, I carried that relationship with beauty through different decades of my life.

Sometimes it felt empowering.
Sometimes it felt exhausting.
Sometimes I didn't even realize how much authority I had given the mirror.

This book is about that journey. Not just mine — but one many women recognize in themselves.

Where the belief begins. How culture quietly reinforces it. How beauty slowly becomes something we feel responsible for maintaining.

And what happens when we finally step back from the chase and ask a deeper question.

Not: How do I stop aging?
But: Why did I ever believe aging diminished my worth in the first place?

Because eventually something shifts. Not dramatically. Just gradually. The mirror doesn't hold the same power it once did.
And one day you realize something unexpected.

The woman in the mirror isn't against you. She's simply what comes next.

Because what matters most was never in the mirror to begin with.

Where It Begins

How It Starts, Often Without Us Realizing

CHAPTER 1

The Seed of Insecurity

The way a woman sees herself rarely begins in adulthood. The story usually starts much earlier – when she is just a little girl.

That girl was me.
I thought I was ugly.
Average at best.
That was the story I carried about myself when I was young.

Not because someone sat me down and said it directly, but because of the comments that floated through the air when I was growing up.

The comparisons.
The compliments directed toward someone else.
The subtle ways a young girl begins to understand where she stands.
Or where she believes she stands.

I thought my sister was the beautiful one.

People said it often. My mother said it often. Not cruelly. But clearly. And when a child hears those distinctions early enough, she begins to file them away as facts.

Pretty.
Not pretty.
Beautiful.
Average.
And somehow, without anyone formally announcing it, I understood where I fell on that spectrum.

Children are astonishingly good observers. They notice tone, reactions, pauses.

They notice which comments are repeated and which are not. Long before they have the language to analyze what they are hearing, they begin organizing the information. And appearance is often one of the first categories.

As a preteen, I would flip through magazines and stare at the girls inside them.

Perfect hair.
Perfect smiles.
Perfect skin.

I remember wondering what it would feel like to look like that.

To be the girl people noticed. To be so beautiful. But that didn't feel like something available to me.

So instead I watched. I compared. I measured.

I quietly assumed beauty was something other girls had simply been given.

Looking back now, I can see that this is how many beauty beliefs begin – not through a dramatic moment, but through a slow accumulation of small observations.

A comment here. A compliment there. A comparison that lands more deeply than anyone intended.

Then came another moment most girls remember. Breasts. Or in my case... The lack of them.

Mine arrived much later than everyone else's. Back then, a lot of girls stuffed their bras with tissues to fake what nature hadn't delivered yet.

I tried it a few times. But the tissues felt scratchy against my skin. So I gave up on the illusion and just lived with the insecurity and the comments that came with it.

I used to spend hours playing with Barbie dolls. Not just dressing them. Transforming them.

Different hair.
Different outfits.
Different looks.

I was fascinated by the idea that someone could create a new version of themselves – a more glamorous version. And once I finally had a makeup mirror of my own, I began experimenting the same way.

Makeup was like a new tool—something that might help me cross that invisible line between average and beautiful.

I didn't think about it too deeply at the time. I just knew I liked how it made me feel.

Looking back, I can see it gave me something I had been craving—visibility.

Before that, I often felt unnoticed. But inside, there was always more. A kind of intensity I didn't know how to show. Makeup felt like a way to express it.

In high school, another way of being seen showed up.

Sex.

It wasn't about rebellion. It was about visibility. For the first time in my life, someone was looking

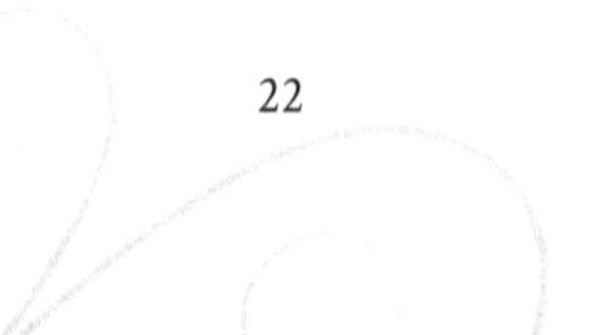

at me in a way that made me feel powerful.
Desired.
Chosen.
And when you've spent years feeling invisible, that kind of attention can feel intoxicating.

The biggest shift didn't happen until I moved away in my early twenties. Leaving home changed everything.

Suddenly the critical voices weren't around anymore. The commentary. The comparisons. The expectations. They were gone.
And for the first time, I could simply be whoever I wanted to be.

It felt like a metamorphosis. I experimented with everything. Hair. Makeup. Clothes. One day I might dress conservatively. Another day I might dress sporty. Another day I might be completely outrageous.

And I loved every minute of it. Because for the first time in my life, I was creating myself and not reacting to someone else's definition of me and living my life through their lens.

That was more than forty-five years ago.

And looking back now, I can see something much more clearly. The messages a young girl hears about her appearance are incredibly powerful.

They settle quietly into the background of her mind. And sometimes it takes decades to question them. Even longer to unlearn them.

When I started looking more closely at where these beliefs come from, I found myself thinking about who I was at my granddaughter's age—what I already believed about myself, and how early those ideas had taken hold.

So I started asking her questions.

At eight years old, Ava doesn't overthink herself.

She's the oldest of three—the big sister to two younger brothers—moving through the world with an easy confidence that isn't trying to prove anything.

Glasses perched on her face, a purple hearing aid she wears without a second thought, nothing about her feels self-conscious or performed.

There's a clarity that's there before the noise of the world sets in.
Before comparison becomes how she measures herself.
Before beauty gets negotiated.
She hasn't learned to question herself yet.

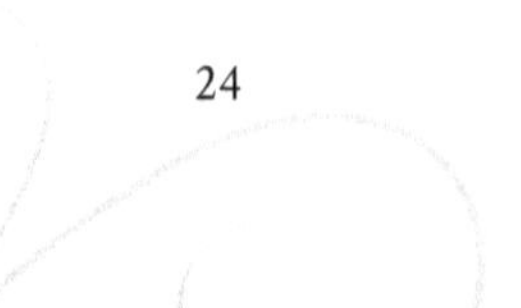

When I ask her what she loves about being who she is, she shrugs a little, almost like the answer is obvious. “I’m nice to people.”

Not because she’s trying to be liked.
Not because she’s been told to be.

Because, in her words, “I want them to feel happy.” That’s it. No strategy. No self-awareness wrapped in performance. Just instinct.

When she talks about when she feels most like herself, it isn’t tied to how she looks or what she’s wearing. It’s simpler than that.

“When I’m with my family...That feels good.”

She doesn’t expand on it. She doesn’t need to. There’s no analysis. No explanation layered on top. Just... that.

And when I ask what makes someone beautiful, she doesn’t hesitate. “When they feel good about theirselves... and when they’re nice to other people.”

It’s not about looks at all.

Not thinner.
Not prettier.
Not more put together.
Just good. And kind.

Even her version of "cool" has nothing to do with appearance. "Cool is being nice to everyone... and helping people." It's almost disarming how simple it is. And yet... it's everything we spend years complicating.

Her perfect day isn't about being seen. It starts simply. "Sleeping in." "Getting donuts." "Going to school—I like school." There's nothing in it that's trying to impress or stand out—it's just what she enjoys, what feels good to her.

And then, without prompting, she adds what matters most.

"No one's fighting on the playground."
"Everyone's nice to each other."
"Everybody takes turns with the equipment."

It's not really about what she's doing, but how it feels—easy, calm, the kind of day where people are kind to each other and things just move the way they should.

The rest of it unfolds the way childhood does—swimming with friends, playing with her family, laughing at stories that don't quite make sense but are funny anyway—and ending the day laying next to her mom in bed, saying her prayers and talking about her day.

It's nothing extraordinary. And somehow... it's everything.

Even when she imagines having a superpower, it's not about control or attention.

"Telekinesis." She wants to move things with her mind. Not to impress anyone—but "to help people lift up heavy stuff." Because it would make things easier for them.

And what makes her laugh the hardest? "When my dad tickles me." Or when she and her friends make up ridiculous stories—like a monster fighting the tooth fairy.

No performance here.
No awareness of being watched.
No pressure to be anything other than what she is.

She doesn't spend a lot of time worrying about how she looks. Some girls might, she says... but she doesn't.

Then she hesitates, "Well, if there's something special like the Daddy-Daughter dance at school—I like to pick out a special dress and have my nails done."

She beams as she tells me this. Smiling, "Yeah, I really like that."

But most days? How she looks is “Fine,” she says with a shrug.

No internal negotiation.
No quiet critique.
Just… no big deal.

When I asked her if there was one thing she could have or change that would make her feel more beautiful… more awesome in her life, she didn’t answer right away.

She actually thought about it. “Ummmm…” Then she giggled and said, “a baby bunny rabbit.”

Not something to improve how she looks.

Not something to make her more put together, or something that the other kids have. Just… a bunny.

Somewhere along the way, we trade that understanding that Ava has for something else.

Not because it disappears—life shows us other ways to see ourselves, and we begin to believe those instead. Children often see something adults forget.

They notice how someone treats people.
They notice kindness.

They notice joy.
And they notice the opposite of these.

In many ways, children are still looking at the world through the lens my grandmother tried to teach me years ago. Beauty isn't just what you see in the mirror. It's what people feel when they are around you.

Often the belief doesn't begin dramatically. It starts with something small.

A comment.
A comparison.
A mirror.
A moment of wondering whether you measure up.
It's a seed.

And once that seed is planted... It has a way of growing.

The beliefs we carry about ourselves take shape slowly—I'm kind, I'm smart, I'm pretty... I'm not—and they can shape the way we see ourselves for decades.

If This Sounds Like You...

Maybe you remember the first time you became aware of yourself through someone else's eyes.

A comment. A comparison. Or a moment in the mirror that suddenly felt different.

At the time, it probably seemed small.
But those moments have a way of staying with us.

Maybe part of you still carries that younger version of yourself — the girl who started wondering if she was pretty enough, lovable enough, noticeable enough. And maybe, without even realizing it, she still shows up in the way you measure yourself today.

In relationships.
In comparison.
In photographs.

In the pressure to keep fixing, improving, or proving something.

Because this chapter isn't really about beauty. It's about the moment awareness begins. The moment a girl stops simply being herself and starts evaluating herself instead.

And the question is...
Do you still see yourself through that lens now?

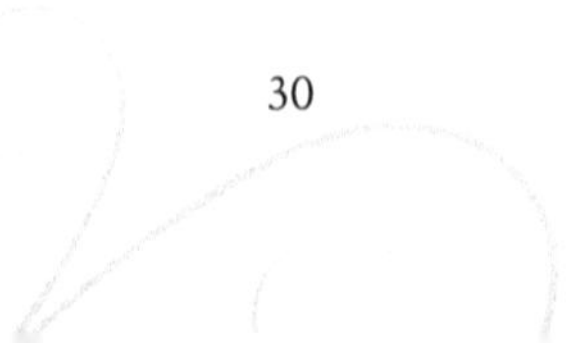

Nothing about us changed—
we just began seeing ourselves
through a different lens.

CHAPTER 2

Hiding in Plain Sight

The beliefs we hold about ourselves rarely arrive fully formed. They grow. Slowly and quietly. Often without us even realizing it.

What begins as a small observation in childhood can become something much larger over time—a story we repeat to ourselves so often that it begins to feel like fact.

Psychologists often describe these early stories as core beliefs.

Core beliefs are the quiet ideas we carry about ourselves and the world. Over time, they shape how we see things and influence the choices we make, often without us even realizing it.

But they don't feel like beliefs when they begin.

They feel like moments.

And for me, one of those moments became something more.

It wasn't just a drifting thought.

It was a core belief.

By the time I reached high school, I felt like I was far behind the other girls who were getting lots of attention—and in my mind, it made sense.

They were taller.
Curvier.
Their bras filled out.
They just seemed older somehow.

I still felt like the same girl in my awkward seventh-grade body. Only now I was a freshman in high school.

It was intimidating.

Not in a dramatic way. Just constant.

I had an unspoken awareness of where I thought I stood. And I didn't like it.

So one day, I went to the store with my cousin with all the babysitting money I'd saved from the summer.

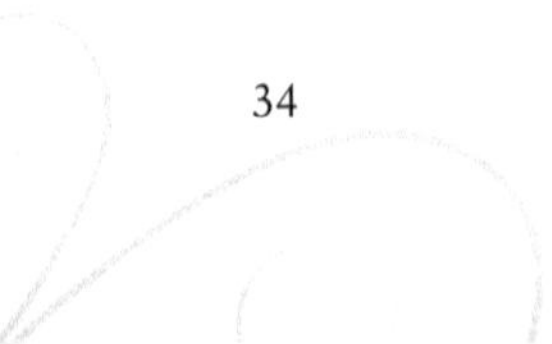

I bought a makeup mirror and as much makeup as I could afford—eyeshadow, mascara, blush, lip gloss. It was 1975—two years before Saturday Night Fever would bring disco glam into the mainstream.

Looking back, maybe I was just a little ahead of my time.

I let my record stand double as my makeup table. I had butterflies as I was setting it all up—like I was getting away with something. Finally, I turned on the mirror, adjusted the lights, and sat down.

I remember the feeling.

The anticipation of what I could do... what I could become...
and most of all—that I wouldn't feel like the same version of myself when I was done.

So I started.

The eyeshadow looked so dark. And the mascara was harder than I expected—my hand was shaking, and it kept smudging. But I kept going.

And when I finished, I just sat there and stared in the mirror.

Something changed. Not dramatically, but enough that I noticed it.

It wasn't just my reflection.

I felt different.

Like I had stepped into something I didn't want to leave.

Then the door opened.
My mom walked in, looked at me, and said, "What's all over your face?"

"Makeup."

"Take it off."

"I like it."

She asked where I got it. I told her—Fashion Fair. With my babysitting money. She looked at me and said, "You look like a floozie."

Then she shut the door.
I sat there in the silence.
Tears coming, mascara starting to run.
My chest felt heavy. And I was sad.

But I wasn't surprised. Mom didn't really wear makeup, other than a little lipstick and mascara. But somehow I felt it was more than that.

I turned back to the mirror.

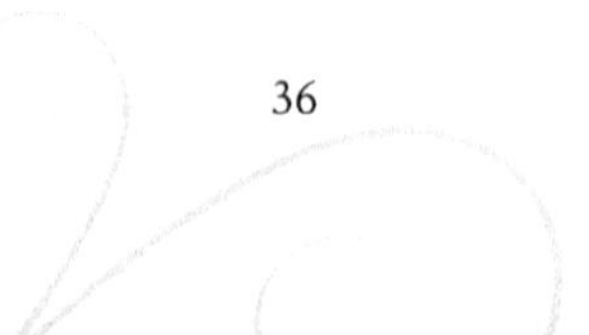

Even with the smudged mascara… I still liked what I saw.

I remember thinking—this feels good.

The next morning, I woke up early and did it again.

When I walked into the kitchen, my mom stopped me.

"You're not wearing that to school."

I didn't argue at first. I just kept making breakfast.

But she kept going—comments about how no one else wears makeup to school. What will people think?

And for the first time, I pushed back.

"Yes they do."

It was small. But it mattered.

When I got to school, my friends noticed right away. They told me I looked pretty. I didn't question it. I just felt it, like they meant it.

And that was new.

Something in me shifted again—not because everything had changed, but because something now felt possible.

And from that point on, I started paying attention.

Looking around at the other girls.
What they were doing.
What seemed to work.

Trying to understand what made someone stand out—and what I needed to do differently to be like them.

Makeup gave me more than a new look. It gave me a way to step outside of what I had already decided about myself.

Because before that moment, the belief had already taken shape.

And after...there was something else. It wasn't certainty—But possibility.

A glance in a mirror that lingers just a little too long. A comment that lands differently than expected. A feeling you don't quite have words for yet—but you remember it anyway.

Core beliefs are rarely formed in one defining moment. They are built through repetition, through small interactions that don't seem significant at the time.

A comment that soaks in.
A comparison that stings a little longer than expected.
A moment of being noticed… or not being noticed at all.

Children don't question these experiences. They absorb them. And because they don't yet have the ability to separate perception from truth, those early interpretations settle in quickly—not as opinions, but as understanding.

I can still picture moments like that.

Standing in a room, aware of other girls without knowing exactly why. Noticing who got attention. Who seemed to be looked at a little longer. Who didn't have to try as hard to be seen.

There wasn't a clear thought attached to it. Not yet, anyway. Just a feeling.

And over time, that feeling started to organize itself into something more defined. Not a dramatic belief. Just a quiet conclusion.

Maybe I'm not that. Maybe I'm something else.

When I was young, my grandmother used to say something to me all the time.

She was the one I went to when I felt sad or lonely. I told her everything— my mom was mad at me, I felt lonely, I didn't think I was pretty.

"Beauty is only skin deep, Shell Bell."

That was her nickname for me.

At the time, I thought I understood what she meant. It sounded like one of those things adults say to kids to make them feel better. But looking back now, I can see she meant something deeper. She wasn't dismissing beauty. She was trying to show me that it wasn't where it ended.

Over time, those small impressions begin to organize themselves into something more permanent. A belief about who you are. Where you stand.

What you can expect. And once that belief takes shape, it quietly begins influencing everything that comes after.

Core beliefs don't just sit quietly in the background. They begin to shape how we interpret nearly everything that follows. They influence what we notice, what we remember, and what we dismiss. They can affect the way we walk into a room, the way we receive a compliment, and even the way we look at a photograph of ourselves years later.

And perhaps most importantly, they tend to stay—not because they are true, but because they have been practiced, repeated, and reinforced.

Not in obvious ways, but in subtle ones.

The way you automatically deflect a compliment, "Oh, thanks, I got it on sale."

The way you hesitate before stepping into a photo, "Wait, let me check my hair."

The way you scan yourself first before anyone else has a chance to.

Over time, these can become so familiar that we stop questioning them altogether. They don't feel like beliefs anymore. They feel like reality.

Once they take hold, the brain begins doing something fascinating: it starts looking for evidence to support them. If a girl begins to believe she isn't beautiful, she may start noticing every moment that seems to confirm that idea—a compliment directed toward someone else, a comparison she overhears, a magazine cover that seems impossibly perfect.

And just as importantly... she begins overlooking everything that doesn't support it.

A kind comment that didn't quite land. A moment she was noticed—but didn't fully take in.

Those moments pass through quickly. But the ones that confirm the belief that she's not enough? They stay.

Over time, these moments accumulate. Not as isolated experiences, but as proof. Proof that the belief must be true.

Researchers who study cognitive psychology refer to this pattern as confirmation bias—the tendency for the mind to notice and remember information that reinforces what we already believe. In real life, it shows up more subtly than that.

It looks like remembering the one comment that stung and forgetting the five that didn't.

It looks like noticing who gets attention and assuming it means something negative about you. It looks like scanning a room and instinctively placing yourself somewhere on an invisible scale.

The brain, in its effort to make sense of the world, quietly becomes a collector of evidence. And once beauty becomes part of that belief system, it can shape the way a woman interprets nearly every reflection she sees.

But personal belief is only part of the story.

If This Sounds Like You...

Maybe there's a belief about yourself you've carried for so long, you no longer recognize it as a belief at all.

It just feels like truth.

Do you automatically assume other women are naturally prettier?
Do you feel like confidence is something you have to earn?
Do you believe being noticed somehow makes you more valuable?
Do you spend more time focusing on what's wrong with you than what's right?

And do you even remember when those thoughts first took root?

Because core beliefs rarely begin in one dramatic moment. They form slowly—through experiences, observations, comments, comparisons — until one day they simply become part of the way you see yourself.

Then you carry them forward.
Into relationships, mirrors, photographs, and the quiet way you evaluate yourself without even meaning to.

Because the beliefs we form early don't just disappear with age.

Most of the time, they grow with us until we finally stop long enough to ask:

Is this actually true? Or is it simply a story I learned so young, it started to feel like a fact?

The beliefs we form early
don't announce themselves—
they quietly become the lens
we see ourselves through.

CHAPTER 3

The Mirror Was Never the Problem

Beauty standards rarely arrive as rules. They move through culture quietly – until everyone seems to believe them.

By the time those early beliefs begin forming, they are rarely developing in isolation.

A young girl is already surrounded by influences quietly shaping how she sees beauty.

By the time a young woman begins forming beliefs about her appearance, she is rarely doing it alone.

She is surrounded by influence.

Friends.
Television.
Magazines.
Movies
Social media.

Each one offering a slightly different version of the same message: this is what beauty looks like. And over time, it starts to feel like truth.

And over time, it doesn't just stay external—it becomes something we start doing to each other.

Because much of the evaluation around beauty actually happens between women.

Women notice details that many men never register.

The haircut, the skincare glow, the subtle shift in makeup, and the dress someone chose for an event.

This isn't necessarily out of competition — although sometimes that plays a role — but because women understand the language of appearance in a way most men simply don't.

Fashion editors have said for years that women often dress as much for other women as they do for anyone else.

Women know the signals, which means they also notice when those signals change.

And beauty standards do change. Constantly.

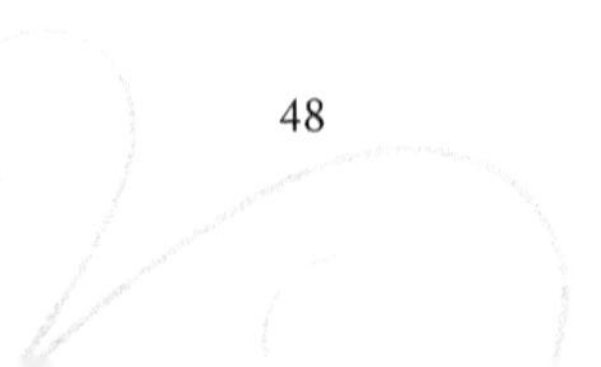

Each generation grows up inside a slightly different definition of what the world calls beautiful.

In the 1950s and early 1960s, elegance defined beauty on screen.

Faces like Audrey Hepburn's became cultural icons — delicate features, defined brows, luminous skin, and a timeless sense of poise.

By the late 1960s, the cultural mood shifted.

Youth culture and rebellion reshaped fashion and beauty alike. Model Twiggy became the unexpected face of the era — wide-eyed, boyish, minimalist, almost the opposite of the polished glamour that came before her.

The 1970s introduced a different kind of look.

The influence of the hippie movement introduced a more relaxed aesthetic — long hair, natural skin, an effortless look that suggested beauty should feel organic rather than constructed. But beauty culture rarely stays relaxed for long.

By the late 1970s and early 1980s, glamour returned with confidence.

Hair grew bigger. Makeup became bolder. Television and magazine culture celebrated a more polished, camera-ready version of femininity. Faces like Farrah Fawcett's helped define that era.

Then the 1990s ushered in the age of the supermodel.

Beauty became sleek, symmetrical, and editorial. Women like Cindy Crawford represented a new kind of aspirational face — confident, polished, and unmistakably photogenic.

Each era subtly rewrote the definition of a "pretty face." And each generation absorbed those signals without even realizing it.

But something fundamental has shifted in the last twenty years.

Beauty used to be shaped primarily by Hollywood, fashion magazines, and advertising. But today it is shaped by algorithms.

The images we see are no longer limited to celebrities. They are everywhere— From friends, to influencers, to strangers on social media. And many of those images aren't entirely real.

Filters smooth skin, adjust lighting, reshape jawlines, enlarge eyes and narrow noses.

With a few taps on a screen, a face can become a subtly perfected version of itself. But the problem is that the brain doesn't always recognize the difference.

Aesthetic providers have begun noticing a pattern in their offices that would have been rare a decade ago.

Patients sometimes arrive with filtered images of themselves and ask whether their real face can be made to match the edited version.

Some physicians have begun referring to this phenomenon as "Snapchat dysmorphia."

Because when someone becomes accustomed to seeing the filtered version of their face every day, the real one can begin to feel unfamiliar.

The mirror hasn't changed.
But the expectation has.

For women who have grown up inside this shift, the awareness often starts much earlier than we realize.

Cassandra is 29, a mother of a three-year-old, and for her, that awareness goes all the way back to fifth grade.

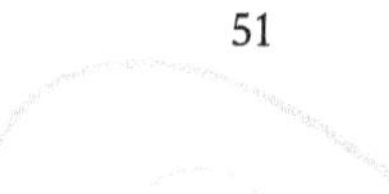

That was the first time she became aware of how she looked—and that it mattered.

“The boys liked other girls. Not me,” she said. “I was chunky. And more of a tomboy.

I remember when I got my first skinny jeans… and lip gloss… then I started brushing my hair in class.

That’s when I started liking boys—and wanting them to like me back.”

Then there was a moment that never left her.

“One day in High School, a boy sitting beside me in class grabbed my leg and said, ‘You have no muscle in your leg.’ And I thought… what? At first I didn’t know what he meant. But that stuck with me.”

From that point on, something shifted.
She went to the gym.
She started paying attention.
To her body.
To how she compared.
To what got noticed.

“When I was younger, I always wanted to have a skinny waist and big boobs,” she said. “I think that came from what I saw in movies.”

And then came real-life reinforcement.

"I remember being 14, and doing promo work with my sister... wearing heels, short shorts, handing flyers out. Guys were coming up, wanting to take pictures with me."

She thinks about it, like it was someone else. "I thought I was the shit. I thought, this is what it means to be beautiful."

That gave her a huge confidence boost and she wanted more.

But looking back now, it lands differently.

"For most of my life, I felt like I wasn't enough. And now I look back and think... I was beautiful. I just didn't know it.

I cry sometimes thinking about it. I can't believe I was more focused on looking good to get the attention of men than just being a kid," she said.

Social media didn't start that—but it intensified it.

"I used to post everything. From sun up to sun down. It was like I wanted people to know me... to think I was cool."

Now, she sees it differently.

"It's all energy when you put it out there. And I'm not looking for that anymore."

Working in the beauty industry, she sees what that pressure turns into for other women.

“I’ve had girls sit in my chair who I barely recognize when they come in.

They look nothing like their pictures.
The filters, the face, the body work...
they’re chasing something that’s not even real.”

She’s made a conscious choice to step outside of that. She doesn’t use filters. She’s had no cosmetic work, but she treats herself to a few facials a year.

And still, she notices how subtle the influence can be.

“There are moments—like when I pull my hair back into a really tight, snatched ponytail and my mom asks if I had Botox—and I catch myself thinking, *oh... is this what I would look like?*”

She loves getting dressed up and going out—but standing there in shoes that hurt and makeup that feels heavy, she’ll catch herself looking at her friend who’s wearing her sweats and tennis shoes, thinking...

“I’d rather feel like that right now.”

And maybe that’s why something else stuck with her.

At home, the message was different. As she watched her mom in her late 30s become deeply committed to her health—training, eating clean, and showing up for herself.

"What stuck with me wasn't how she looked. It was how she felt. She was happier."

That became the part she carried forward.

"Now I feel strong and healthy because I take care of myself. And that gives me confidence. I love being strong."

She seems relieved realizing she doesn't want the skinny waist and big boobs that she used to think was the goal.

"I didn't even know what confidence was back then. I thought it came from how you looked... or who noticed you."

Now, it's something else entirely.

"Every woman should have something she feels good about. It all goes back to loving yourself... and talking gently to yourself."

And today, when the old thoughts creep in–and they do–she catches them.

"If I start questioning if I'm beautiful or if I'm enough, I stop and think... someone else is probably looking at me, saying, I wish I was her. We all do it."

This is where beauty culture becomes especially powerful. Because the comparison is no longer just between ourselves and celebrities.

Now we are comparing ourselves to curated versions of people we know personally—Friends, family, coworkers, and neighbors.

There's the woman from high school whose life suddenly looks perfect online. It is a comparison landscape previous generations never had to navigate.

And the human brain – wired for comparison – steps right into it.

Am I prettier than her?
Do I look as good as she does?
Why is my skin less vibrant?
Why does my face look different?

The questions rarely arrive consciously.
They hover, almost unnoticed, beneath the surface.

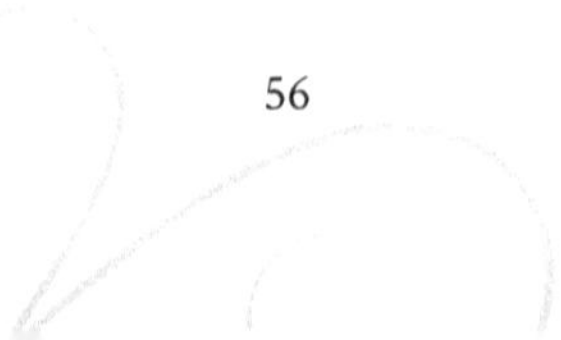

And once that comparison cycle begins, it becomes surprisingly difficult to step outside it.

Beauty culture has a way of doing something subtle but powerful.

It turns appearance into something we believe we should be managing—Constantly improving, maintaining, or optimizing.

And when that happens, the mirror stops being just a reflection, and it becomes a scorecard.

If This Sounds Like You...

Maybe you've changed parts of yourself over the years without even realizing why.
Your clothes, your makeup, your hair.

Do you ever buy something because you genuinely love it...
or because it helps you feel more current, attractive, or accepted?
Have you ever looked at another woman and immediately questioned yourself?

Do you feel different depending on who you're around?
Have you ever followed a trend you didn't even like that much just to avoid feeling out of place?

Maybe the way you present yourself shifts depending on what seems to be "in."

And maybe some of it genuinely felt fun and expressive. But maybe some of it came from something quieter – the desire to fit in, keep up, stay current, or feel more acceptable in the eyes of other people.

Because trends don't just influence what we buy. They influence what we believe looks good.

They influence what feels desirable and what makes someone seem confident, relevant, and attractive.

And after a while, it becomes hard to separate what you actually like from what you've simply learned to admire.

Maybe you compare yourself more than you mean to.
Maybe certain women make you question yourself for reasons you can't fully explain.
Maybe part of you is exhausted from always feeling like there's another version of beauty you're supposed to keep up with next.

The truth is, beauty standards keep changing. They always will.

But what if the version of you underneath all of it was never the problem to begin with?

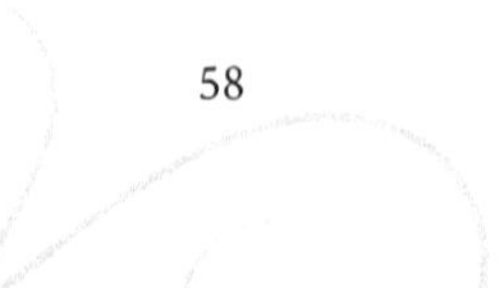

When the standard
of beauty keeps shifting,
the chase rarely ends.

How It Grows

The Influences, The Patterns, And The Pull

CHAPTER 4

Beauty Is a Business

Beauty may feel personal. But behind the mirror sits an industry.

Most women grow up believing their relationship with beauty is personal – a matter of taste, expression, or preference.

Makeup.
Hairstyles.
Clothing.

And skincare routines often feel like individual choices that simply evolve over time.

But the environment surrounding those choices is anything but personal, it is commercial.

Beauty is one of the largest consumer industries in the world. Global estimates place the beauty and personal care market at well over $500 billion annually, with skincare and anti-aging products among the fastest-growing sectors.

Entire segments of the industry are devoted to helping people maintain or restore a youthful appearance.

Creams promise smoother skin.
Serums promise renewal.
Treatments promise correction.
Devices promise tightening and lifting.

Once I clicked on an ad for an anti-aging serum, and from that moment on, it felt constant.

Every scroll—another product, another solution, another reminder.

The algorithms don't forget. They just keep reinforcing it like a subliminal message programming your subconscious... don't forget you're getting older... what about those crow's feet?

Yet, many of these products and treatments do deliver real results.

Skin can improve.
Hair can become healthier.
Lines can soften.

Dermatology and aesthetic medicine have made remarkable advances over the past few decades.

But the deeper structure of the beauty industry is not built around permanent solutions.

It is built around maintenance. Think about it—If a cream erased wrinkles forever, you would never need another jar.

If a single treatment permanently stopped the visible effects of aging, entire parts of the industry would disappear.

Because the beauty economy thrives on routines — products and services designed to be used and repeated over time.

Hair color appointments every six or eight weeks.
Nail fills every few weeks.
Lash maintenance.
Daily skincare regimens that stretch from morning into evening. This is typical.

Each step seems small on its own and none appear to be extreme. Over time, however, these routines accumulate, and what once felt like occasional self-care can begin to feel like it requires constant attention.

It's something most women around you are doing... Something normal. And normalization is one of the most powerful forces in consumer behavior.

The beauty industry rarely tells women directly that they need something.

Instead, it introduces possibilities.
A new product.
A treatment that promises subtle improvement.
A technique that offers a slightly fresher appearance.
And the message is rarely dramatic, it is incremental.

You could look just a little better.
And maybe a little better after that.

Over time, those small improvements become part of a broader culture of maintenance.

Women begin to talk not just about looking good, but about maintaining results –
preserving youthfulness,
staying refreshed,
keeping up with the version of themselves they still recognize.

Researchers who have studied consumer spending on beauty estimate that women may spend tens of thousands – sometimes well over $100,000 – on beauty products and treatments over the course of a lifetime.

This spending builds gradually across decades of routines that feel ordinary at the time.

What once began as occasional upkeep in our forties now often starts decades earlier, quietly extending into years of habits and costs that accumulate long before we stop to question them.

This is precisely how the system is designed to work. And inside that system... There are people who see it up close every day.

She has spent most of her life in and around beauty—first behind counters, then in treatment rooms.

Kathryn is 56, a mom, a grandmother, and a licensed aesthetician and laser technician.

She's someone who now sits across from women every day, watching what brings them in... and what gradually keeps them coming back.

There's a groundedness to her. She understands it deeply—but she isn't pulled under by it either.

She's sees about seven to ten women a day, and what she's learned over time is that it almost never begins the way people think it does.

It doesn't start with wanting to look different...
It usually starts with something small. Curiosity, mostly.

"Usually it's microneedling," she tells me. "It's affordable, and they're really pretty informed when they come in."

By the time they sit down in her chair, most women already know just enough to feel informed... and just enough to be interested.

It feels harmless.
Almost as common as getting a facial used to be.

Most are just dipping their toe in the water—something small, something manageable... it doesn't feel like a big decision yet.

But even in that first step, there's already a quiet awareness of what else is available.

"Most of them will say they just want to look refreshed. Just a little. Nothing drastic."

"I think they just want to turn back the clock a little bit... and look more natural. Especially the older women—they want to look like themselves again."

There's something tender in that... reaching back toward familiarity.

But she's also watching a different version of this take shape.

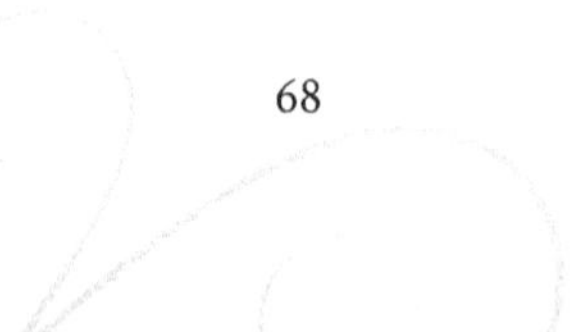

"The younger ones are different," she tells me.

"They're very savvy. They've done a lot of research, and most of what they're seeing—their ideas, their references—it's all coming from social media. And often… they're not trying to look like themselves."

They have an idea in their mind—and they tend to be harder on themselves.

That shift—from returning to yourself to subtly becoming someone else—doesn't happen all at once.

It unfolds in small ways.
And once someone steps into it, there's no single path forward.

What she's seen is that there's no prescribed process once someone steps in.

Some women go all-in right away and stay there with regularly scheduled appointments, just like having their hair touched up.

Others move in and out of it—they take a break, they come back after a while. Some settle into a kind of maintenance routine.

"People prioritize what matters to them," she tells me. "Some will even skip vacations to do treatments."

And it isn't always about vanity. Sometimes it's about value. And over the years, she's watched it all expand.

"There's definitely been an uptick in procedures," she says.

"I'm definitely seeing more people, younger people, and a lot more men. It's just more acceptable now."

What once felt occasional has become increasingly expected.

"You feel like a therapist half the time," she says.

What comes out in that room isn't just treatment requests. It's reflection.

"Self-talk says a lot," she says.

"When it's very negative... when they say things like, 'I don't like how I look,' or 'I'm aging so badly,' and you look at them and you don't see that, you know you can't change that."

And she's not outside of all of this.

"The aging process is hard," she tells me. "And I'm okay with that... I've let go of a lot of it. But I still want to look and feel as good as I can."

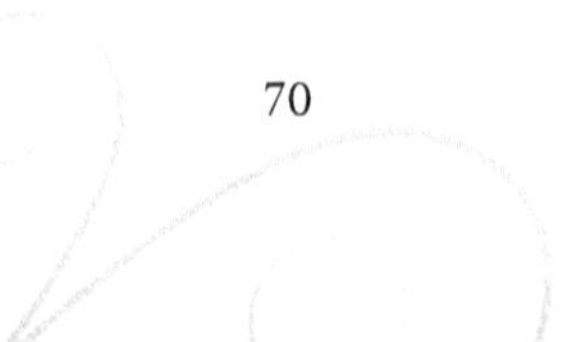

"I think I'm harder on myself because of it... the pressure of being in the industry. Because you want to stay relevant."

When everything else is stripped away—after the treatments, the conversations, the years of watching this up close—what she comes back to is something much simpler.

"I can't fix whatever's going on in your life," she says.

"I can help you feel better for a little while... but I can't fix that part."

And then, just as quietly—
"You're going to age regardless of what you do."

"And finding that acceptance sooner rather than later... will save you a lot of heartache."

The truth is, most beauty routines do not begin with dramatic decisions. They begin with something small. Something reasonable. And sometimes something that isn't even cosmetic at all.

Which is exactly how it began for me. My introduction to Botox had nothing to do with beauty. It was migraines.

If This Sounds Like You...

Have you ever told yourself it's just a little maintenance?
Just one product?
Just one treatment?
Just trying to look refreshed?

Have you ever felt pressure to "keep up" without fully realizing when it started?
Did your routines slowly become expectations?
Has your reflection ever started to feel more like a project than a person?

Do you compare your face now to versions of yourself from five, ten or twenty years ago?
Do social media, ads, filters, or beauty trends influence how you see yourself more than you want to admit?

Have you ever wondered whether you truly want these things...
or whether aging simply started to feel like something you were supposed to fight?

You are not alone.

And maybe this chapter isn't asking you to stop caring about beauty at all.
Maybe it's simply asking you to notice something.

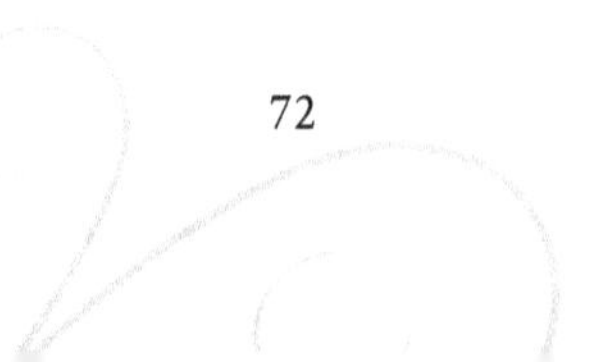

How much of your attention has been shaped by an industry designed to keep you searching for one more improvement… and what if there was never anything wrong with you to fix in the first place?

It doesn't begin with a decision—
it begins with something
that feels justified.

CHAPTER 5

Catching the Bug

For most women, the shift from simply caring about how we look to actively trying to improve it doesn't happen all at once. It happens gradually, often through small, reasonable decisions that seem harmless at the time.

My introduction to all of this didn't start with lines on my forehead.

It started with the pain of headaches.

I remember one of the first times it really hit.

I was sixteen, on a bus headed to a state-wide high school competition. I hadn't felt well that morning, but I told myself it was just nerves.

I wasn't a fan of trying new things, and I had gotten carsick for as long as I could remember. So I had already built it up in my mind that I might feel sick riding the bus.

Turns out... I wasn't wrong.

Soon after we boarded the bus, my head started pounding. Not a headache—something sharper. Like it was splitting open from the inside.

I wanted to close my eyes, but I didn't dare. I knew that would make me dizzy or nauseous... or worse. So I sat there. Trying to hold still. Just trying to keep it together.

Somehow, I made it through the two-hour bus ride and reluctantly checked in for the competition. All I can remember is the room. It was huge with bright lights.

Lights that didn't agree with me in any way.

All I wanted to do was find a bathroom and hide until it was time to get back on the bus and go home. But I didn't.

Soon enough, the proctor explained the rules, set a timer, and told us to begin.

So I did.

I sat there for hours, trying to focus through the pounding in my head, the overwhelming nausea, and the feeling that something wasn't right—but I pushed through anyway.

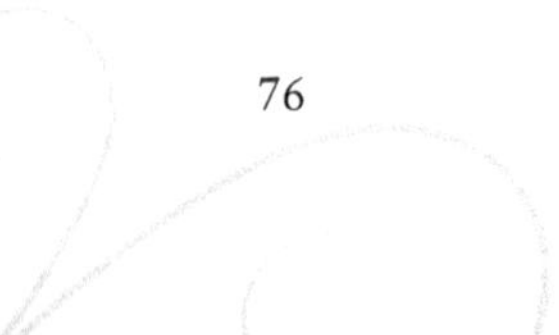

Two and a half hours later, I finished the test.

Then I went straight to the bathroom and threw up.

Then came the wait—hours for the awards ceremony. Everyone gathered in the bleachers as I sat there with my head in my hand, barely able to keep my eyes open, just praying it would be over soon.

When I heard my name, I thought it was a mistake.

First place? I should have been happy but I wanted to cry.

I could barely see straight, yet somehow I had won first place?

Afterward, I boarded the bus, holding my head still, with my trophy in my lap, just trying to make it through the ride home. I didn't have a name for it yet, but looking back, that was the beginning.

Decades of migraines ahead.

There were so many familiar triggers.

Perfume.
Storms.
Staying up too late.

Certain foods.
Hormones.

Things I learned to anticipate, but never fully control.

By the time I was in my early forties, they had taken over my life. I was in bed at least three days a week, completely unable to function.

The other days, I was functioning—but medicated and just getting through.

And even on the days I went to work, it didn't mean I felt okay.

I would sit at my desk under fluorescent lights that felt like they were piercing my eyes... trying to focus and push through.

Some days, I would get up, walk to the bathroom, and give myself a rescue injection—just to take the edge off enough to get through the rest of the day.

Then I'd go back to my desk like nothing had happened, praying for the day to end.

Some days, I would leave early, drive home, walk through the door, and fall straight into bed with an ice pack pressed against my head.

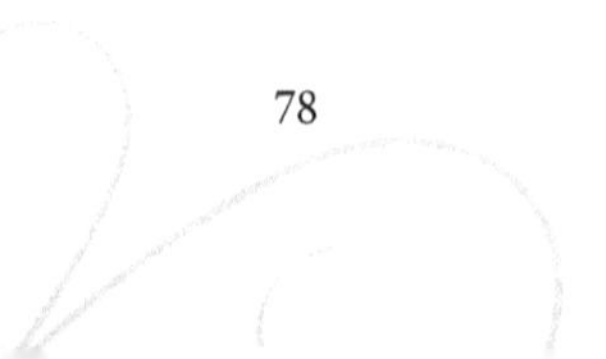

That was my life.

At one point, my doctor put me on birth control pills to try to regulate the headaches.

He said they were caused by fluctuating hormones.
The pills didn't help.

What they did do was make me gain ten pounds in two months and I felt like hell.
That was the moment I said—no more.

I was forty-two.
My tubes were tied.
I wasn't planning to have more children.

Yet I was on birth control to try to manage migraines that were still landing me in bed several days a week.

There were so many days the kids would come home from school, hoping to find me in the kitchen—my happy place—baking cookies.

Instead, they would tiptoe down the hall and find me in the dark, with an ice pack over my eyes.

That was my life.

And that was when a friend mentioned a study at the Mayo Clinic using Botox as a treatment for migraines.

I remember thinking—at that point, I'll try anything. So I did. Mayo referred me to a neurologist, and off I went.

Every twelve weeks, like clockwork, I showed up for my appointment.

I got my injections.
I felt the relief.
Then it was back to life as usual.

And the difference didn't take long to show up. Within the first week, I noticed it.

Less intensity.
Less frequent.

By four weeks, the change was dramatic. The migraines didn't disappear completely, but they dropped enough that I could feel the shift in my entire life.

My energy picked up. I felt lighter. And happier.

I felt more like myself than I had in a long time.

Not just surviving the day... but actually in it.

And looking back now, those shots didn't just help the pain.
They gave me my life back.

They gave my family their life back. So I kept it up. And over time, I started to notice the pattern.

Around week ten... maybe eleven... there would be a slight shift. A few more headaches, more intense pain—a reminder. A signal that it was wearing off.

And I would think, *Okay... it's time.* It didn't feel like dependence. It felt like staying ahead of something that used to control my life. It was my new maintenance routine.

There was never any conversation about beauty at my appointments either. At least not yet.

Then one day, it happened.

I went in for my usual treatment, and when I stepped up to the front desk to check out, the receptionist looked up and said:

"That will be $2,100."
"What?!?"
I assumed she had made a mistake.

Up until that moment, insurance had been covering the injections since they were considered part of my migraine treatment. But somewhere along the way the game had changed.

Despite the relief Botox had given me, my insurance had decided it was no longer an approved treatment for migraines.

Just like that, something that had once been medically necessary became optional—cosmetic—and very expensive.

That moment unknowingly changed the direction of my journey.

Instead of continuing through the neurologist, at an outrageous out-of-pocket cost, I soon found myself sitting in a very different kind of office for my migraine relief—a med spa.

The environment felt different immediately—less clinical, more aesthetic—and the conversation began to shift. Instead of costing thousands of dollars, it was hundreds.

At first, the injections were still about migraines. I was guiding the injector based on where my neurologist had been placing them.

But gradually, the suggestions started appearing.

"Have you ever considered a little filler here?"
"Your nasolabial folds could soften with just a small amount."
"Sometimes people add a little volume to the cheeks."

Nothing dramatic... just subtle tweaks. Tiny improvements.

At that point I was in my mid-forties, and like many women in their forties, I had started noticing small changes in my face—the slight hollowing in the cheeks, lines forming where the skin used to be smooth.

Things I had never really paid attention to before.

But there was more to it than that. It was shortly after I had lost my husband. I had been through a lot.

Grief has a way of showing up everywhere—even in your face.

I had lost weight.
I looked tired.
Drawn.
Like something in me had dimmed.
I didn't feel like myself.

So when I found myself sitting in this new environment—the softer lighting, the mirrors, the shift in conversation—it didn't feel like something new.

It felt like I was already in it before I understood it.

In that moment—sitting there, hearing those suggestions—it didn't feel like vanity. It felt like relief. Like maybe I could get a piece of myself back.

Why not just a small amount? Just to see.

The result was immediate.
The hollow area softened.
The lines faded.
And when he handed me the mirror, I saw something familiar—a version of myself I recognized.

A little more rested… a little more alive.

I looked a little more like who I used to be.

And in that moment, it felt like exactly what I needed. At least… that's what I told myself.

Then came the comments.
"Did you do something to your face?"
"You look great."
"You look so refreshed."

And suddenly something clicked in my brain. It felt strangely familiar.

Like when I put on makeup for the first time again. I felt visible.

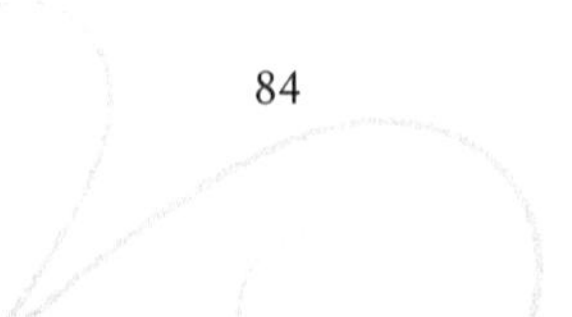

For many women, that moment of being noticed carries more emotional weight than we realize.

Psychologists who study identity and appearance have long observed that positive feedback about attractiveness can influence how people evaluate themselves.

Compliments activate the brain's reward pathways, releasing dopamine—a neurotransmitter associated with motivation and reinforcement.

Dopamine doesn't just make us feel good at the moment. It encourages the brain to repeat whatever behavior produced the reward.

In other words, the brain connects the dots quickly and this is how it goes:

Change appearance. Receive approval. Feel good.

And when that loop forms, it can become surprisingly powerful.

Researchers who study social validation have found that approval from others can influence behavior just as strongly as many other forms of reward.

The difference is that appearance-based validation is woven into everyday life—compliments from friends, comments from coworkers, subtle shifts in how people respond.

Most of us never think of those moments as reinforcement, but the brain does.

Which helps explain why cosmetic improvements can feel so compelling.

The reward isn't just what someone sees in the mirror—it's how the world responds to it.

At the same time, these treatments are quickly becoming more common.

According to the American Society of Plastic Surgeons, minimally invasive cosmetic procedures have increased dramatically over the past two decades.

Millions of injectable treatments—including Botox and dermal fillers—are now performed every year in the United States alone, with women representing the vast majority of patients.

Botox has become the most frequently performed cosmetic procedure in the country.

Part of its appeal is how simple it appears.
The treatment itself often takes less than fifteen minutes, there is little to no recovery time, and the results are subtle enough that most people simply look refreshed.

That subtlety has changed the way people think about cosmetic treatments.

Instead of dramatic transformation, the focus has shifted toward maintenance—

Softening a line before it deepens.
Refreshing tired eyes.
Keeping small changes from becoming larger ones.

For many women, the goal isn't to look different. It's to look like themselves—but just a few years younger—an earlier version.

And when the results are subtle and the compliments begin arriving, the decision to continue can feel perfectly reasonable.

Let's Be Honest...

Before we go any further, I want to be transparent about where I stand. By no means am I standing on the outside of this whole conversation about beauty.

I wear makeup almost every day.
I color my hair.
I get my nails done regularly.
I wear fake lashes.

And I got breasts implants at 27 to satisfy what my 12-year-old self had determined was inadequate.

So let's not pretend I've renounced beauty culture entirely.
I haven't. If anything, I've lived right in the middle of it. And I still do.

So this isn't a story about rejecting beauty.

It's about recognizing when the pursuit of it quietly begins to take up more space than it was ever meant to—and learning how to put it back in its proper place.

Looking back now, I can see how easy it was to slide into that pattern without fully realizing it.

Nothing about it felt extreme at the time. It just unfolded through a series of reasonable decisions—a treatment that worked, a small improvement, then a compliment, and another adjustment.

And somewhere along the way, the line between caring for your appearance and managing it begins to blur.

Because what begins as curiosity slowly becomes routine—almost expected.

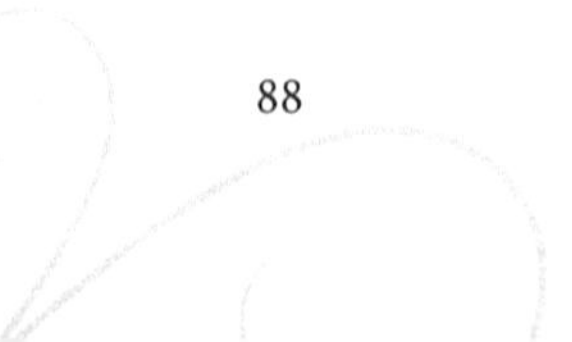

And routine has a way of making things feel normal—even when, at the beginning, they were never part of the plan.

Most beauty routines don't begin with a dramatic decision.

They begin with one small step that feels completely justified at the time.

And it doesn't happen all at once. It happens so slowly, and you don't even realize you're in it until you are.

If This Sounds Like You...

If you've ever been having a terrible day...
feeling exhausted, insecure, invisible, or just off...
and then someone says,
"Wow... you look really good today," and suddenly your entire mood shifts...

If you've ever noticed how one compliment
can stay with you longer than an entire conversation...

If you've ever caught yourself asking a friend,
"What are you doing differently?"
or wondering how someone suddenly looks so refreshed, glowing, or youthful...

If you've ever started thinking,

Maybe I should try that too...
Maybe that's what would help me feel better...
If you've ever believed—
even for a moment—that fixing something on the outside
might finally quiet something on the inside...

You are not shallow.
You are human.

But maybe it's worth asking yourself this:

How much of the way you feel about yourself is actually coming from you... and how much is coming from the reaction you hope to receive from everyone else?

It never starts big—
it starts small, and then it sticks.

CHAPTER 6

Keeping It Together

There's a season in a woman's life where everything begins to converge.

Not dramatically, and not all at once—but slowly, steadily—until one day you realize you're managing more than you ever expected to.

Your life, your relationships, your responsibilities, your appearance... all at the same time.

And somewhere in that, a quiet expectation forms—that you should be able to hold it all together.

Not just functionally, but visibly.
Seamlessly.
Gracefully.
As if nothing is slipping.
As if nothing feels heavy.
As if everything is exactly as it should be.

This is the stage where identity starts to stretch.

You're no longer just becoming—you are responsible for what you've built. A home, a family, a rhythm, a life that others now depend on.

And with that comes a different kind of awareness.

Not the early awareness of being seen, but the ongoing awareness of how you are perceived—how you show up, how you look, how your life looks, how it all appears from the outside.

Because by this point, it's not just about you anymore.
And yet somehow... it still is.

She's 35, married, a mother of three—and my daughter—building a life that, from the outside, looks full in all the ways that matter.

But like so many women in this stage, what's visible is only part of the story.

She remembers that at first, beauty was just something you heard.

She was very young. "You're so cute, you're just so cute." Words that didn't carry much meaning—until they did.

Around eight or nine, when conversations about crushes started, she began to understand that

how you looked could influence how you were seen.

"That's when it clicked," she says. "That looks actually mattered in some way."

Growing up in the early 2000s, the messaging didn't have to be direct to be powerful.

It was everywhere.
Media.
Movies.
Magazines.
Beauty meant thin.
Beauty meant visible.
Beauty meant chosen.

"You just kind of infer it," she explains. "You see it enough, and you know what it means."
And yet, she doesn't remember being defined by it. "I was mostly confident," she says.

What grounded her more was how she was seen beyond appearance.

"I didn't feel like there was a big emphasis on how I looked. It was more that I was smart, a good reader... those were the things I identified with."

That began to shift in her teenage years, when the outside noise got louder.

Body image became part of the conversation, and thinness became something to pay attention to. At the same time, she was watching what was modeled at home—not as pressure, but as an example.

"I remember when my mom really got into working out and taking care of her body," she says.

"It didn't feel like pressure—it felt like, oh, this is what you do. You take care of your body. You want to feel strong, healthy... you care about yourself."

That awareness didn't disappear as she got older. It evolved.

In her twenties, it showed up in effort.
In her thirties, it became something quieter—but more constant.

"Now it's my skin, wrinkles, and my postpartum body," she says.
"Before it was my weight, how I looked in clothes... it's always something—it just changes."

Over time, the pressure didn't just come from what she saw—it came from what she knew. What was available. What other women her age were doing.

She's experienced that side of it—the treatments meant to enhance. Botox, and other treatments...

the subtle things that promise to smooth, lift, or hold things in place.

"It felt good at first," she admits, "but at the same time, I felt like I didn't look like myself."

Her expressions felt different. Her smile didn't land the same.
"That's what stuck with me."

So she stopped. Not dramatically, and not with a statement. Just a decision.

But the thoughts don't disappear, they just shift.

"It's not that I want to look like someone else," she explains. "It's more like... if everyone else keeps doing more, and I don't, what does that look like over time? Will I fall behind?"

There's a fear in that—not panic, not insecurity in the traditional sense.
Just an awareness of the pace.

What's becoming normal, what's available, and the choice not to do all of it.

Motherhood added another layer to it.

"You don't have the same amount of time. You don't have the same energy. And your body isn't the same," she says. "But you're still expected to show up like it is."

That expectation isn't always spoken, but it's felt.

"When I'm going to meet people for the first time, that's when I feel it more," she says. "You want to put your best foot forward."
And when she doesn't do that?

"But if I'm being honest, it's more like... I could have."

Not judgment—just awareness.
And then, something shifted.
Not in how she looked, but in how she saw herself. Her understanding of beauty began to root itself somewhere deeper—in her relationship with God.

"There was a point where I realized He doesn't need my performance," she says. "He already sees me as enough."

That didn't remove the awareness, but it changed the weight of it.

And if she could say something to other women in this stage—women balancing motherhood, identity, and everything in between—it wouldn't be about doing more.

"Instead of drowning in comparison," she says, "spend your time and energy finding ways to accept yourself and love yourself.

Dig into why you feel the need to conform... and instead just be your authentic self."

And this is where the shift happens.

What she's describing isn't just about appearance—it's about the unspoken pressure to hold everything in place. Your life, your identity, your responsibilities, your body... all at once.

And somewhere in that, it becomes easy to believe that how well everything is "together" is a reflection of how well you're doing.

But it's not. Because most of what we're trying to hold together was never meant to be held that tightly—not your body as it changes, not your life as it evolves, not your identity as it expands.

And the pressure doesn't disappear just because you're aware of it...

It just becomes easier to see. Which means you get to decide what actually matters... and what you're done carrying.

Maybe the shift in this season isn't learning how to manage your life and your appearance—It's realizing you don't have to.

If This Sounds Like You...

If you've ever felt like you're carrying everything at once...
your family, your work, your relationships, your responsibilities...
while also feeling pressure to still look put together through all of it...

If you've ever looked around and thought,
How is everyone else keeping up?

If you've ever felt guilty for not spending more time on yourself...
and then guilty when you do...

If you've ever gotten ready to leave the house
and felt the pressure to look like your life is more together
than it actually feels sometimes...

If you've ever noticed
that the standards seem to keep moving...
and no matter what you do,
there's always something else you could improve...

If you've ever worried
that everyone else is doing more—
aging slower, looking better, keeping up easier—
and wondered what happens if you stop trying to keep up...

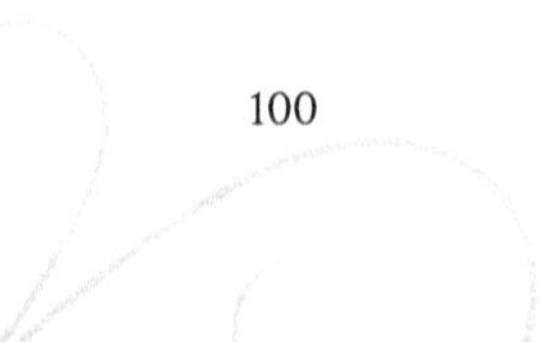

If part of you is exhausted
from feeling like you have to manage everything perfectly
while pretending it all feels effortless...

You are not failing.
You are living inside a culture that quietly taught women they are supposed to hold everything together beautifully.
But maybe it's worth asking yourself this:

What would change
if you stopped measuring your worth
by how well you appear to have it all together?

Keeping it together isn't the goal.
Understanding what's been
shaping it… is.

CHAPTER 7

The Quiet Game of Comparison

Beauty doesn't stop at the face. At some point, the pressure women feel about appearance expands to the entire body.

Weight, shape, skin, and muscle tone.

Every part of us becomes something to evaluate. Something to improve. Something to control.

And for many women, that awareness doesn't arrive dramatically. It develops gradually.

First through comparison. Then through comments.

Then through the subtle realization that bodies—especially women's bodies—are constantly being measured against some invisible standard.

Beauty standards for women have never been static.
They shift with time.

With culture.
With trends.

What one generation celebrates, the next often replaces with something entirely different.

And nowhere is that more obvious than in the expectations placed on women's bodies.

When people talk about beauty icons from earlier generations, Marilyn Monroe is often part of the conversation.

There has always been debate about what clothing size she actually wore. Some sources estimate she wore a size 10. Others suggest a size 12.

But the interesting part isn't the number.

It's what those numbers meant at the time.

In the late 1950s, a woman with measurements close to Marilyn Monroe's—roughly a 34-inch bust and a 25-inch waist—was considered a U.S. size 12.

Today, a size 12 typically fits someone closer to a 39-inch bust and a 32-inch waist.

In other words, the standards themselves have slowly shifted.

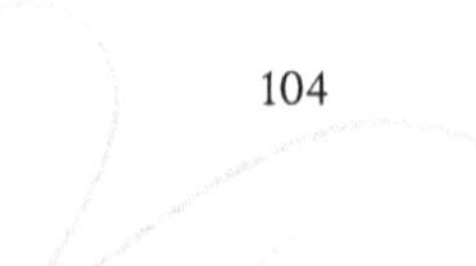

Not loudly.
Not all at once.
But gradually… covertly… until what once felt extreme started feeling normal.
What used to be labeled a 12 might now be called a 6 or an 8 in many clothing brands.

Retailers didn't redesign the human body… They adjusted the labels.

The fashion industry even has a name for this phenomenon: vanity sizing.

Clothing sizes have gradually been relabeled over the decades to make shoppers feel better about the number on the tag.

Which raises an uncomfortable question. If the numbers themselves are arbitrary—and have been adjusted repeatedly over time—why do so many women give them so much power?

Most of us know someone who has secretly cut the size tag out of their clothing so no one can see it.

No judgment here.
Because we've all seen it.
Or maybe we've even done it ourselves.

This psychological relationship between numbers and self-worth isn't accidental.

In 1954, psychologist Leon Festinger introduced Social Comparison Theory, which explains that people naturally evaluate themselves by comparing their traits and abilities to those around them.

In earlier generations those comparisons happened mostly within small social circles like friends, neighbors, or family.

Today those comparisons happen against global images—

Celebrities.
Influencers.
Filtered photos.
And curated online lives.

Research on body image consistently shows that repeated exposure to idealized images increases body dissatisfaction, particularly among women.

The body itself hasn't necessarily changed. But the standard has.

What the mirror is to our face, the scale often becomes to our body.

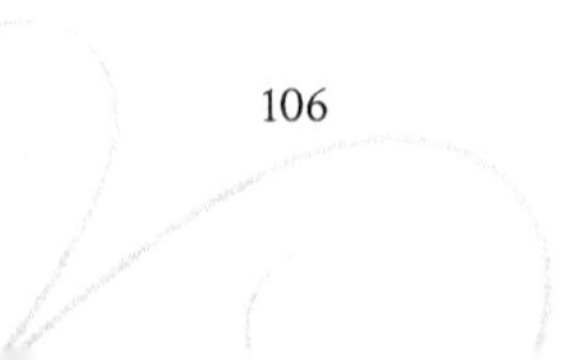

And for many women, the number on the scale determines whether the day starts out good or bad.

They may never say it out loud,
but that number keeps running in the background of their mind all day—like an app quietly draining the battery on a cell phone.

Sometimes that number has more influence over her mood than anything else that happens that day.
And yet the scale tells us almost nothing about the things that actually matter most about our bodies.

Like strength.
Endurance.
Or health.

It doesn't tell us anything about cholesterol, blood pressure or heart rate.

And it certainly doesn't measure character.

But culturally, we've allowed it to become a kind of emotional scoreboard.

And over time, that scoreboard doesn't just track the body—it shapes the way we think about ourselves.

And it rarely feels like competition. It feels like awareness—like noticing something that needs adjusted without even realizing it.

The comparison game doesn't always announce itself through the mirror or the scale.

Sometimes it shows up the moment we walk into a room and suddenly feel out of place.

Not thin enough.
Not polished enough.
Not dressed right.
Not quite aligned with whatever the room seems to expect.
And in those moments, it's interesting how quickly confidence can change—not because of who we are, but because of how we think we compare.

A while back, I was invited to a fundraising event for a non-profit organization I was working with.

I tried to get a sense of what the attire was for the event, but I was only able to connect with a few of the men organizing it, and their answer was simple:
"Dress warm. You'll be outside."

It was an informal setting at a Mexican restaurant and club in the uptown area. Our table was on the patio near the fire pits.

I invited my girlfriend Lori as my plus one to the event. I decided on jeans, tall black boots, a bodysuit, and a leather jacket… perfect for a chilly outdoor evening.

As we were walking up to the restaurant, I stopped cold—I couldn't believe my eyes.

It was a cocktail formal event. I had never seen more sequins, satin, and stilettos in one place since New Year's Eve.

Lori and I looked at each other, shocked. But then immediately started laughing.

Then came the quick strategy conversation—do we go home and change, arrive late, get back in the car and go for tacos, or just deal with it and walk in like we own the place?

We decided to walk in and own it.

We had a great time. But something funny happened.

I noticed how many times throughout the night we apologized for what we were wearing. How often we said we "didn't get the memo."

And what stood out the most for me wasn't how I looked.

It was how I showed up.
At an event like that, I would typically be mixing, mingling and connecting.

But that night, I stayed close to home base. I didn't venture far from the fire pit.

And I didn't show up as the extrovert I knew myself to be.

I didn't play the ambassador role for our nonprofit the way I should have. All because I showed up casual while everyone else was full-glam and camera-ready.

That was about seven years ago. Since that time, I've been in a similar situation at another event. It was another moment where I realized I didn't get the dress code.

But this time, something was different.

I didn't shrink like last time.
I moved through the room.
I engaged with people.
I complimented their dresses.

I felt energized.

I thought about it afterward...
It wasn't the setting that had changed. It was me.

The first time, I felt small.
The second time, I felt secure enough to simply be there.
Same situation.
Different relationship with myself.

Because so much of how we experience ourselves in a room comes down to how we think we compare at that moment.

Kristin described this shift in a way that makes that relationship easier to see. The shift didn't start in the mirror for her. It started in the way she talked to herself.

She's 48, a mother of four and a new grandmother. For most of her life, the way she thought about her body felt completely normal.
The quiet self-criticism.

The constant awareness of her weight, and the underlying sense that her body needed to be managed.

It was so familiar she never questioned it. Until her life coach interrupted her pattern—and called her out.

"You're better than that."

She remembers going home and sitting with it, asking herself, "Am I better than that?"

That question opened something.

It led her into deeper work, and eventually into something she had never practiced before: self-compassion.
Over time, what changed wasn't her body—it was how much space it occupied in her mind.

In her earlier years, even in the middle of raising children, there was always an underlying awareness of how she looked and what needed to be improved.

And the more attention she gave it, the worse she felt.

Now, that internal dialogue is largely gone.
She no longer talks about dieting or calories.
She doesn't frame exercise as something to offset what she's eaten.

Instead, she moves because she wants to take care of herself—a walk with a friend, time outside, staying strong.

The purpose shifted.

And with that shift came something unexpected: confidence.

It wasn't because she changed how she looked, but because she stopped making her body the central measure of her worth.

There was a time when attractiveness meant the obvious—body, clothes, image.

Now, she defines it with one word: Magnetic.

Her take is that the woman who is fully herself is attractive.

The one who isn't curated or polished, but real.

She's drawn to women who are open, unfiltered, even a little messy—the ones who will say, "*I'm having a shitty day*," instead of pretending everything is fine.

Not perfect. Just honest.

She also describes seeing other women differently now.

Less through the lens of appearance, and more through energy—whether someone feels open or guarded, present or performing.

The external markers matter less.

When she looks back at photos of herself ten years ago, she doesn't see a better version of her body. She sees stress, inflammation, and exhaustion.

What she notices most is a body carrying more than it was meant to.

She was doing everything "right," but operating in constant pressure. As she put it:

"It wasn't my body—it was the pressure I was carrying in it."

Now, she feels healthier and more like herself—not because she's doing more, but because she's carrying less.

Less pressure.
Less comparison.
Less self-criticism.
Along with more awareness.
More acceptance.

And much more compassion.

If she could offer one piece of guidance to women coming behind her, it wouldn't be about weight or appearance.

"Pay attention to how you speak to yourself. Because that conversation shapes everything that follows."

This is where the shift becomes visible. Not when the body finally changes—but when the pressure around it begins to release.

What Kristin experienced isn't about doing more.

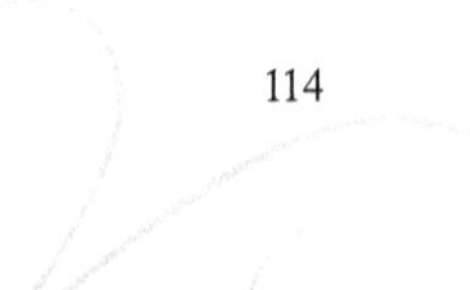

It's what happens when the constant evaluation softens—when the body is no longer treated as something to fix, but something to live in.

And maybe that's the part we miss.

Not that the body needs to change—but what happens when the relationship to it does.

If This Sounds Like You...

If you've ever let a number on a scale, a clothing tag, or a pair of jeans decide what kind of day you were going to have...

If you've ever stood in front of a mirror immediately scanning for what needs to be smaller, tighter, smoother, or different...

If you've ever compared your body to another woman's without even meaning to...

If you've ever walked into a room and suddenly become hyperaware of yourself—your clothes, your weight, your age, your appearance—simply because of who else was there...

If you've ever felt confident one moment...and completely unsure of yourself the next based only on comparison...

If you've ever spent more time criticizing your body than appreciating everything it carries you through...

If you've ever believed that confidence would finally come once your body looked different...

You are not alone.

Because for so many women, comparison became so normal we stopped recognizing it as comparison at all. It just started to feel like awareness.

But maybe it's worth asking yourself this:

What would happen if you stopped treating your body like a problem to solve... and started treating it like a place you deserve to live in peacefully?

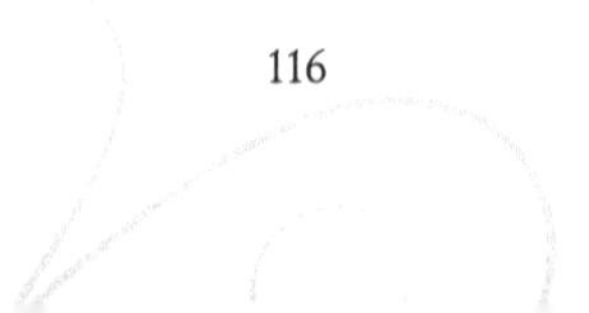

The standard keeps changing.
Maybe the problem was never
our bodies at all.

CHAPTER 8

What Men Think—and What We Do With It

I watched a scene from a movie a few years ago that I still think about. Two men were sitting on a park bench.

They looked to be somewhere in their mid-sixties—both a little overweight, both balding, their clothes rumpled in the comfortable way that suggests they had stopped worrying about impressing anyone a long time ago.

They were simply sitting there, talking, relaxed and at ease.

A young woman walked by. She looked to be in her late twenties or early thirties, wearing a short skirt and walking with the confidence that often comes with youth.

As she passed, one of the men leaned slightly toward the other and quietly said,
"Her ass is too big."

The other man chuckled.

And the conversation moved on.

It was such a small moment—a throwaway comment.

But something about it stuck with me, because the contrast was impossible to ignore.

Two aging men—clearly far removed from the physical standards society expects of women—casually evaluating the body of someone young enough to be their daughter.

You couldn't miss the irony.

And the more I thought about it, the more I realized the scene felt familiar—not because of those two men, but because the dynamic behind it shows up everywhere.

Moments like that illustrate something women have been navigating for generations. Appearance isn't judged equally—not across genders, not across age.

Men are rarely expected to remain visually youthful in the same way women are.

A man in his sixties with gray hair, wrinkles, or a soft middle is often described with words like distinguished, seasoned, experienced.

Aging, for men, is framed as an accumulation of character.

For women, it's frequently framed as a loss of value.

This shows up everywhere—in movies, advertising, leadership, and dating.

It's not uncommon to see male actors in their sixties cast opposite female love interests many years younger—sometimes decades younger.

The message is subtle, but clear:

Men age.
Women maintain.
Or at least try to.

But what's more interesting than how men see women... is what women start to do with that.

Because whether we realize it or not, most women grow up understanding that they are being looked at—not just seen, but evaluated.

Not just noticed, but measured.

And over time, we don't just experience that.
We participate in it.
We start watching ourselves the same way.

We don't just walk into a room—we check ourselves in it.

We might even pay attention to what we're wearing.

How we're standing.
How we look when we laugh.
How we might be coming across.

It becomes automatic, and it pulls you out of your own life, because part of you is always managing how you're being seen.

It even shows up in ways we don't question.

We say we're getting dressed "for ourselves," but most of us learned what that even means through other people's eyes—what's flattering, what's appropriate, what gets attention, what doesn't.

That voice didn't start with us.

But we carry it.

We say we care what men think.

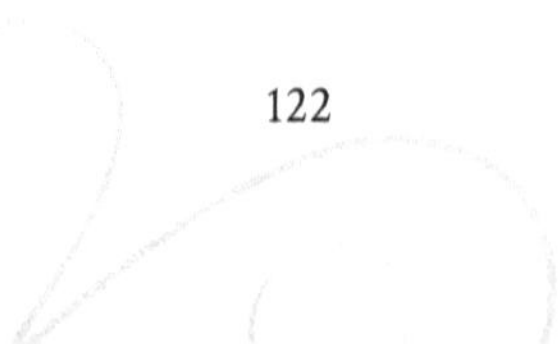

But long before that, we were watching each other.

It didn't start with being noticed. It started with observing—quietly, consistently, without even realizing we were doing it.

Magazines spread out on the floor.
Pages turned slowly.
Faces studied, not with judgment, but with curiosity.
We didn't question what we were looking at.
We just absorbed it.
This is what beauty looks like.
This is what you're supposed to be.

And it wasn't just celebrities. It was girls at school, friends, older girls who seemed more put together, more confident, more... finished.

We noticed how they did their makeup, how their clothes fit, what seemed to work. Not in a deliberate way—just over time, through repetition.

Somewhere in that, something began to take shape.

We weren't just looking anymore—we were measuring.

Not against men, but against each other. Trying to understand where we fit, what we needed to change, how to close the gap.

And at the same time, something more complicated was happening.

We admired them. We wanted to look like them.

And whether we admitted it or not—
there was a quiet edge of jealousy underneath it.

You hear it all the time.
Women sitting across from each other at lunch—

"Oh my God, I love your dress. Where did you get it?"

It sounds like a simple question. But she's not taking a survey of online shops. She's wondering if it would do the same thing for her that it does for you.
"Wow, you look amazing."
"You look great."

And we mean it.
But underneath it... there's often something else.
A quiet comparison.
A subtle pull.

A thought we don't say out loud—
Would that work on me?

Not in a harsh way.
Not in a competitive, obvious way. But it's there.

And whether we admit it or not, it pushes us.

To try something different, to adjust, and to figure it out.

So we keep watching, and keep adjusting. We keep trying, in small ways, to move closer to what we think we're seeing.

It didn't even feel competitive. It felt like learning—like we were picking up on the rules of what made someone stand out, what didn't, and what seemed to matter.

By the time men's opinions entered the picture, something had already been established.

A standard.
A reference point.
An internal scale we were already using.
So when a comment came later—"You look amazing," "Wow, you look great"—it didn't land on its own. It landed on top of something that had been building for years.

That's why it carries weight.

Not because it's the first opinion, but because it either confirms or challenges what we've already started to believe.

We say we want to be attractive.

But if you look closely, what we're often trying to be is recognizable—aligned with something we've seen before, something that fits.

Because long before anyone was evaluating us, we were already evaluating ourselves—through the lens of other women.

I know I did. For years, I would walk into a room—or even a date—with a quiet thought running in the background:

I hope they like me.

I hope he thinks I'm attractive.
I hope I say the right thing.
I hope I measure up.

So much of my attention was directed outward.
How am I being perceived?
What impression am I making?
Am I enough?

But somewhere along the way, something shifted.

Now when I walk into a room, the question is different.

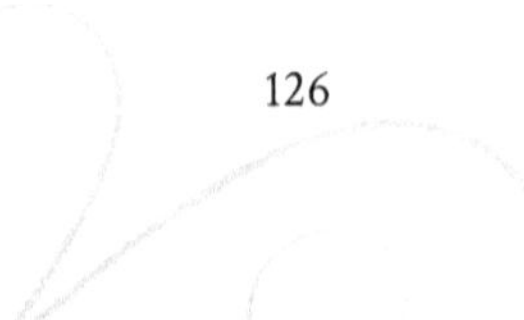

Do I feel like myself here?
Am I comfortable?
What's my energy here?

So the focus moved—from approval to awareness. And that shift changes everything, because when you stop trying to be liked, you start trusting what you feel.

By the time I moved into my sixties, I had experienced something I hadn't before—what it feels like to spend real time on your own, with no one there to shape how you see yourself.

Just you... and a clearer sense of who that is.

And how different it feels when you're not constantly adjusting for someone else.

So when I started dating someone new—someone who mattered to me—it felt different. But not in the way you might think.

I was still doing the same things I had always done—dressing up, hair done, makeup just right—the usual routine of getting myself ready the way I always had.

That part of me hadn't changed yet. But something about him was different.

The connection felt more real... more grounded.

We had long, easy conversations, the kind where you lose track of time.

We laughed till it hurt. It didn't feel like we were trying to impress each other, and it felt like we weren't wasting time.

He wasn't focused on the physical the way many men were.

He talked about what he saw in my eyes... the layers beneath the surface of who I was. And his attention stayed there. I couldn't help but notice that.

Even if I wasn't completely used to it...
or entirely comfortable with it yet.

At first, I almost didn't trust it. Because it felt unfamiliar—not being measured in the same way. There was nothing to adjust for, and nothing to fix. Just... being there was enough.

Then one day, he said something that stopped me.

"You know you don't have to get all dressed up. It's nice... but you're beautiful just being yourself. Your confidence—that's what makes you sexy."

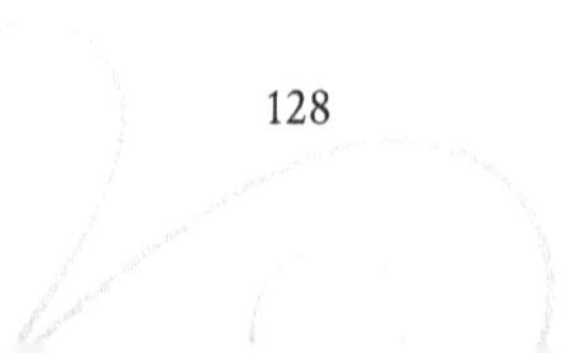

We talked more about it after that—not just once, but over time.
We came back to it from time to time.
I told him how I had always felt like I needed to try harder.

To stand out.
To be more.
To get it right… to be perfect.

How somewhere along the way, I had connected that effort to being noticed, and to being wanted.

And his perspective—that it wasn't necessary, that it actually got in the way—was a relief I didn't even know I was looking for.

It reminded me of how I used to feel years ago… back in my "mom" years—like I could just be myself.

It felt familiar. But this time, it meant more.

There was something powerful about having someone show up 30 years later… and remind me of this.

And now I had the life experience to really understand it… to feel the depth of it in a way I couldn't have before.

That version of me—the one who didn't feel like she had something to prove. And for the first time in a long time, I was remembering her.

We talked about that too.

About how much I had been trying... and how I didn't need to. I remember feeling like I was able to exhale.

It didn't change me overnight.
But it made me pause.
Because for the first time in a very long time, I could feel it.
That I was more than what meets the eye. Not someone constantly trying to prove I was enough.

And over time, I started to settle into that. To believe it a little more each time he reflected it back to me—reminding me what he saw inside.

Slowly, the checking softened.
The second-guessing quieted.
The self-criticism started to fall away.
I wasn't stepping into a room wondering how I was being perceived anymore.
I was just in it.

As it turned out...the new awareness stayed.

And so did the relationship.

And maybe that's why that park bench scene stayed with me. Not because it was shocking. But because it made something clear.

A lot of what women feel about themselves isn't something they consciously chose.
It's something they learned.

And that begs the question:
How much of your life has been shaped by someone else's opinion of you...
and who would you be without it?

If This Sounds Like You...

If you've ever walked into a room
already wondering how you were being perceived...

If part of your attention
was always focused on how you looked,
how you sounded,
how you were coming across,
or whether people found you attractive...

If you've ever adjusted yourself—
your clothes, your makeup, your personality, your energy—hoping to be liked, wanted, chosen, or enough...

If compliments from men

or approval from other women
felt more powerful than you wanted to admit...
If you've ever compared yourself to another woman and immediately wondered
what she had that you didn't...

If you've ever spent years trying to become
more attractive, more polished, more impressive...
only to realize you still didn't fully feel secure...

If you've ever confused attention with worth...
or effort with lovability...
You are not alone.

Because most women were taught to see themselves through someone else's eyes long before they ever learned how to see themselves clearly through their own.

But maybe it's worth asking yourself this:

Who would you be
if you stopped constantly evaluating yourself
through the possibility of someone else's approval?

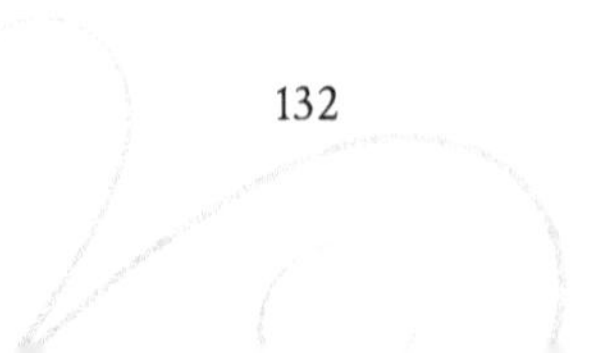

At some point, you have to decide whose voice you trust more—yours, or everyone else's.

Seeing It Clearly

The Shift From Reaction To Awareness

CHAPTER 9

Redefining Beauty

At some point in life, many women begin asking a different kind of question.
Instead of How do I look? the question becomes: *Why does this matter so much?*

For years, the mirror quietly trains us to keep asking the first question.
How do I look today? Do I still look like myself? Do people notice?

Those questions can follow a woman for decades. They show up in dressing rooms, in photographs, in passing reflections caught in store windows or car mirrors.

They appear when we see an old picture of ourselves and notice how different we looked years ago, or when we catch sight of someone who seems to be aging effortlessly and wonder what they're doing that we aren't.

For a long time, those questions feel normal. And even expected.
And no one teaches you to question them. They're just there... running quietly in the background.

But eventually, for many women, something changes.

The mirror slowly stops being the center of the conversation, and a different kind of awareness begins to surface.

Sometimes it happens over time—through experience, getting older, and seeing life differently than you once did.

Other times, it comes from the realization that chasing the perfect reflection is endless. Because there will always be something.

Another line.
Another product.
Another treatment.
Another "fix."

The goalpost doesn't stay still. It moves, and it will continue to.

This realization began for me around 60. At some point, I started asking myself a different question: What am I actually chasing?

Because the truth is... our lives were never meant to revolve around appearance alone. Yet the cultural conversation often suggests otherwise.

Women are taught—directly and indirectly—that maintaining beauty is part of maintaining value. The message is:

Stay youthful.
Stay attractive.
Stay relevant.

It's subtle, but it's constant. And over time, it becomes something we don't just hear—it becomes something we believe.

But eventually, you begin noticing things you didn't pay attention to before.

Not just what someone looks like, but the way they carry themselves, the way they move, the energy they bring into a room—their presence, warmth, and confidence... And so much more, like their humor, and depth.

These are the things you only notice when you slow down enough to really notice someone.

And once you start seeing people that way, something else begins to happen.

The focus on appearance starts to loosen a little.

Not all at once. But enough to realize beauty was never just about what you saw in the mirror.

Especially in a culture that moves quickly—where first impressions often become final judgments—most people never stay long enough to see beyond that. Or give someone

a second glance.

But that deeper presence? That's the kind of beauty that actually stays.

I learned that in a much deeper way after leaving a relationship that had slowly drained something out of me emotionally.

By the end of it, I had stopped seeing possibility in my life. Everything felt heavy.

I felt consumed by someone else's anxiety, negativity, and constant overwhelm.

And I didn't even realize how much of myself I had lost until I left.

When I look back at pictures from that time, I don't even recognize myself. I see a woman with beautiful skin, perfect cheekbones, and hollow eyes. It's a woman who looked fine from the outside, but didn't feel alive inside.

And then something changed.

Once I left, it felt like the lights slowly came back on. I started feeling hopeful again. I was interested in life and excited.

Suddenly, I could see possibilities where before I only saw obstacles.

And interestingly, that's when people started saying:

"You're glowing."
"You seem lighter."
"You're shining."

What people were responding to wasn't perfection. It was relief.

Hope.
Lightness.
Presence.
And energy.

I've always noticed that happiness shows up in ways that go far beyond a smile.

I had a good friend—I'll call her Kelly—who was stunning. The kind of woman people noticed immediately. She had flawless skin and beautiful features.

She was always polished and put together. She kept up with every new procedure, treatment, and enhancement. We used to joke that she looked like she belonged on the cover of a magazine because she always seemed camera-ready.

But something about the picture never fully matched who she was. Because she wasn't happy. Not with her job, her husband, her house, her dogs, or her housekeeper.

There was always something wrong. Something disappointing... something irritating.

Complaining had almost become a sport for her.

And even though she photographed beautifully, I noticed something every time we took pictures together.

The smile was there. But it felt disconnected from the rest of her expression.

Her eyes never seemed to join in. Everything looked rehearsed and controlled. Almost frozen.

Because real happiness shows up differently. You see it in the eyes and the softness of their expression, and the warmth they carry.

And you can feel it in the energy they bring into a room. You can tell when someone is genuinely lit up from within.

But the "say cheese" smile is different. It feels practiced. Or performed.

Sometimes it's emotional disconnection. Sometimes it's exhaustion. Sometimes it's years of trying to hold everything together while convincing the world you're fine—or trying to appear happy when you're not.

And sometimes, if we're honest, years of cosmetic treatments and enhancements can make it harder for the face to express emotion naturally.

But beneath all of that is something deeper.

Many women spend years chasing what they believe will finally make them feel happy, confident, worthy, desired, or enough. The perfect face. The perfect body. The perfect version of themselves.

All while overlooking the thing that actually changes how someone looks most:

Joy.
Peace.
Purpose.
Connection.
Hope.

Because true beauty doesn't just live in the structure of someone's face. Eventually, it reveals itself in the life behind it.

Lisa is 61, and she's clear about how she approaches aging.

"I don't want to just let it happen," she told me. "I want to fight it every step of the way." She laughed when she said it—but she meant it.

She does it all—Botox, fillers, injections, body sculpting.

For her, these aren't extreme measures. They're part of how she takes care of herself.

Her sister sees it differently.

"She says she wants to age gracefully," Lisa told me.

"And I always say… this is my version of graceful."

For her, it's not about chasing perfection. It's about feeling good when she looks in the mirror.

She says it makes her feel like herself, and confident in her own skin. And she's very intentional about it.

"I'll keep doing it as long as I can," she said. "As long as it makes me feel good."

Aesthetic treatments exist for a reason. They give women options—the ability to choose how they want to age, how they want to feel, and how they want to show up.

And for many women, that choice feels empowering. This isn't about judging that.

It's about understanding it and looking at it through a different lens. Because the same decision—to maintain, enhance, or change something—can come from very different places. There's pressure, expectation, habit, and genuine preference. And those aren't the same thing.

That shift doesn't mean you stop caring about your appearance. It means it stops being the center of your identity. It stops being the thing that defines your value.

And when that happens, something else takes its place.

You start thinking differently about your time, your energy, and your life.

And maybe that's what redefining beauty really is. Not rejecting beauty, but changing the importance we give it.

If This Feels Like You...

Have you spent years believing happiness, confidence, or peace would finally arrive once you looked better... younger... thinner... smoother... more beautiful?

Have you ever looked at someone who seemed flawless on the outside and quietly realized they still didn't seem happy?

Have you ever smiled in pictures while feeling disconnected inside?

Have you ever focused so much on maintaining an appearance that you lost touch with how you were actually feeling?

Have you ever mistaken looking alive for actually feeling alive?

And when you think about the people who feel the most magnetic to you... are they usually the people trying the hardest to appear perfect?

Or are they the people whose energy, warmth, confidence, humor, and presence make you feel something deeper than appearance ever could?

If part of you is beginning to realize that beauty may matter far less than you were taught it did... you are not alone.

Because eventually, many women begin to understand something important:

Beauty can enhance a life, but it cannot create happiness, peace, connection, purpose, or self-worth on its own.

And maybe that's the real shift.

What if the goal was never to stop caring about beauty entirely...
but to stop needing it to carry the weight of your identity?

The shift happens when
your opinion of yourself matters
more than anyone else's.

CHAPTER 10

Acceptance

Aging has a way of asking questions that youth never needed to answer.

When we're younger, the questions are simple and immediate.

How do I look?
Am I attractive enough?
Do people notice me?

For many women, the mirror quietly trains us to keep asking those questions for decades. It becomes something we check, adjust, and measure ourselves against—so consistently that we stop realizing we're doing it.

But eventually, something begins to change. The questions don't disappear, but they begin to shift.

At some point, it stops being only about how you look and becomes something else entirely. Am I still myself?

It's a question many women feel but rarely say out loud, because underneath it isn't just appearance—it's identity.

Over time, the way we see ourselves becomes tied to what is reflected back to us—not just in the mirror, but in attention, feedback, and subtle reactions from the world around us.

It's what is noticed, what is praised, and what is reinforced that all shape how we understand who we are.

So when that reflection begins to change, it doesn't just feel like something physical is shifting. It can feel like something personal is shifting too.

And sometimes that realization doesn't come gradually. It comes in a moment.

For me, one of those moments happened in a grocery store line. I had been standing there for about ten minutes, just people-watching while I waited. There were several people in line, and the man in front of me was easily in his seventies. I was in my mid-forties at the time.

The cashier looked young—seventeen, maybe eighteen. But definitely not twenty-one.

So for some reason, the thought popped into my head—not in a creepy way, but in a "I almost feel his age" kind of way.

Because even then, at 45, I felt twenty-six. And in a lot of ways, I still do. Not because I think I look twenty-six, but because that's how I experience myself.

That's just the energy I move through the world with. I can't really explain it. But that part of me has never really changed.

So when the cashier—Jeff—looked at me and said, "Ma'am, next," I didn't respond. Not because I didn't hear him. Because I didn't realize he was talking to me. I actually looked around, assuming there was someone else behind me.

And then it hit.

He meant me.

I placed my groceries on the check-out and watched him scan them. I thought about the man in front of me and wondered if he saw me the same way—as a ma'am.

Jeff bagged my items, I paid, and left—but I carried that moment with me.

I told my girlfriend about it and joked about it with my kids. But underneath the humor, something had shifted. It became one of those quiet before-and-after moments in life.

Before, I wasn't a "ma'am."
After... I was.
And in the background of my thoughts, a question started to form.

Am I a ma'am?
Am I old?
Do I look like a ma'am?

It sounds small. But it wasn't. It was a crack in identity. Because nothing about how I felt had changed. But something about how I was seen had.

And once that question is introduced, it doesn't just disappear. It lingers.

I used to think this would ease with time. That at some point, you just... settle.

That you stop noticing every little thing.
Stop adjusting.
Stop caring so much.

But when I looked at my mom's story, I realized that might not be true. She was in her seventies.

And she was still thinking about it.

Her bangs were thinning, and she talked about it all the time—adjusting them, checking them, trying to make them look fuller. Asking about products. Pointing them out in pictures.

Then After my dad passed away, she got braces—she was 72. Her whole life, she had smiled with her mouth closed to hide her teeth. They weren't perfect, and somewhere along the way, she decided that was something she needed to hide.

So she did.

Then later, she had her eyes done so she wouldn't need glasses anymore. She thought she would look better without them. But it didn't go as expected.

Without the glasses, she saw something else instead—the lines and wrinkles around her eyes, that her frames had been hiding all those years.

So she went back to the eye doctor and had clear lenses put into her frames so she could wear her glasses again. She didn't need them to see. She needed them to soften the imperfections she suddenly couldn't stop noticing.

Those stood out to her far more than her true beauty.

And watching that... It shifted something for me. Because it wasn't about age. And it wasn't about fixing something once and moving on.

It was the same pattern—still repeating, even at seventy.

And patterns don't resolve on their own.
They just keep going—unless something interrupts them.

And then there are moments that don't just make you question things—but they change the way you see the answer.

For me, that moment came in an unexpected way.

One day recently, out of curiosity, I dropped a photo of myself into an AI aging app and asked it to show me what I might look like at eighty—16 years forward. I expected to laugh. Maybe even cringe.

Instead, I found myself staring at the image longer than I expected.

At first, I was simply curious, studying the details—the thinner skin, the lines around the eyes and mouth, the softness that replaces the sharper edges of youth. Wondering how accurate it was.

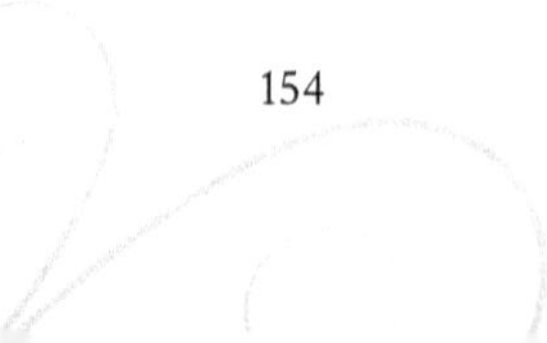

But what surprised me most wasn't the image, it was my reaction.

It wasn't fear.
It wasn't rejection.
It wasn't the reaction I had trained myself into over the years.

You know the one. You take a selfie and the lighting is unforgiving, the lines look deeper, the skin looks tired—and the response is immediate. Ugh. Or sometimes... nope. Delete.

I have done that more times than I can count. There was even a stretch of time when I stopped taking selfies altogether—it felt easier not to see it.

And I wondered if other women did the same thing—take the picture, look at it, judge it, and delete it. Almost like we were editing ourselves out of existence one photo at a time.

But this time was different. I didn't want to delete the image. I didn't cringe. Instead, I leaned in with curiosity.

And that's when I saw it so clearly.

My grandmother's eyes.
My granddaughter's sparkle.

Generations of familiarity, all held in one image.

I kept looking—not with judgment, just curiosity. I saw thin, finely wrinkled skin. Lips that had given thousands of kisses and lines that told the story of decades of laughter.

It wasn't just a face. It was a life.
A face shaped by years of loving people,
years of laughing, years of showing up.
And suddenly it became very real.
The woman in that image wasn't a stranger.
She was me.

And inside that eighty-year-old woman, every part of me still existed.
The girl who laughed too loudly.
The one who felt invisible.
The one who wondered if she was pretty.
The young mother holding babies on her hip.
The career woman building something,
proving something, becoming something.
The woman who lost her husband and had to learn how to stand again.
The woman who kept going.
The one sitting with here today.

We don't become different people as we age. We become more complete.

We carry every part of ourselves forward, like chapters added to a book—not erased, just expanded.

And when you see it that way, something shifts. Because aging doesn't take you away from yourself. It reveals everything you've lived.

Rejecting that woman would have felt like rejecting part of myself. It wasn't something I consciously decided—it was just a natural sense of acceptance.

Because she didn't feel like a stranger. She felt familiar, like a version of me I simply hadn't met yet.

And now, for the first time, instead of holding onto who I had been, I was willing to meet who I was becoming.

If This Sounds Like You...

Have you started realizing that aging is not something you can outrun?

Do you feel the tension between wanting to hold onto youth and wanting to make peace with where life is naturally taking you?

Have you wondered how much time, energy, or emotional space you want to keep giving to the fear of getting older?

When you look at older women, do you notice the difference between those who seem comfortable in themselves and those still at war with time?

Have you started questioning whether acceptance might actually feel lighter than constantly trying to stay unchanged?

Is part of you beginning to understand that growing older is not a personal failure?

What if aging is not something to hide?
What if beauty can evolve instead of disappear?
What if peace matters more than preservation?

And what if true acceptance is not giving up on yourself at all... but finally realizing there is more to life than trying to hold onto youth forever?

Aging doesn't take you away from yourself—It brings you closer.

CHAPTER 11

The Moment You See It

It's easier to recognize it in someone else before you're willing to see it in yourself.

She's standing in a dressing room, turned slightly toward the mirror, smoothing the fabric across her waist.

She pauses, studies it, adjusts it again, then steps back as if distance might offer a different answer. Her attention stays focused on one small area, narrowing in as though something needs to be fixed before she can move on.

Nothing about it looks dramatic. There's no frustration, no visible insecurity—just focus. It's quiet, persistent, and familiar.

A few minutes later, she walks out and asks, "Does this look okay?" It sounds like a simple question, the kind people ask without thinking.

But the answer isn't really what she's after. You can hear it in the tone. It isn't about the dress—it's about confirmation, about closing the loop that started in front of the mirror.

And sometimes, even before anyone answers, you can see it in her face. She's already decided. She's just waiting to hear if someone else will confirm it.

Then there's the photo.

Everyone leans in, the moment unplanned. Before anyone else reacts, she reaches for the phone. "Let me see." Her eyes go straight to herself. She zooms in slightly—not to take in the picture, but to study it. There's a pause, a small shift in her expression.

"Delete that one."
No one says anything. Everyone gets it.
And once you start noticing it, it's hard to unsee.
I still do it.

Whenever I have an event to go to, I'll usually pull a few outfits I'm considering and try them on. I stand in front of the mirror, deciding which one I like and which feels right.

And then I ask him, "Does this look okay?"

This isn't new for me. I've done it my whole life.

In the past, I was used to hearing things like, *that's pretty... I like that... that's sexy*—responses that were easy, affirming, and predictable.

But now, with him, it's different. He's honest—which is what I always said I wanted. Still, the first time it happened, it caught me off guard.

"That's nice... but it's a little formal."
"I like that, but you kind of look like one of the event planners."

He wasn't harsh. He wasn't trying to hurt me. He was just being honest. Exactly what I had asked for.

But in that moment, I felt something sink in me. What surprised me most was how quickly it affected me.

Right there, I felt it.
And I had to sit with it for a moment.
Why did that hit me so deeply?
What exactly did it trigger in me?

Because it wasn't about the outfit. I could still decide to wear it. Nothing had actually changed. But something else had. And it didn't take long to recognize it.

It felt familiar.

Like I was six years old again, believing I wasn't pretty.

But when I look back on it now, my mom never actually said those words.

That was a conclusion I came to on my own.

Because other people were. And because I heard more about how I could improve than I ever did about simply being enough.

And somewhere in that, I decided that pretty just wasn't something I was.

A story I had carried since childhood. It wasn't loud, or constant. But it was there.

And in that moment, it showed up again—only now it wasn't coming from her. It was coming through the voice of a man I trusted who was simply being honest.

Not unkind.
Not critical.
Just... factual.

But I had been conditioned to hear something else from partners—to expect reassurance and approval. And more importantly, to expect a version of the truth that felt better.

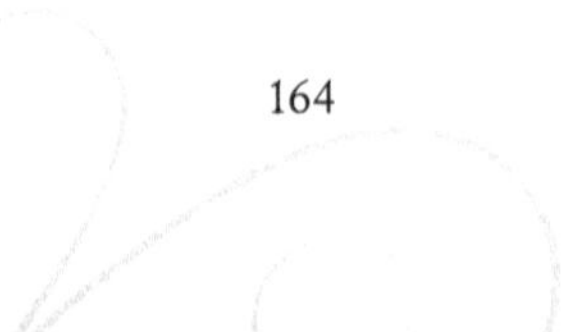

So I sat with it.
Later, I picked up my journal and started writing. And I didn't stop. Page after page, working through what had actually happened—not in that moment, but underneath it.

The reaction wasn't about him. It was about something much older. It was a voice I had heard before. A belief I had formed long ago and carried for decades.

It was something that had been sitting beneath the surface, waiting for the right moment to show up again. And that's when I saw it. Once you notice it there, you start to see it in other women in other places.

At dinner, she's in the middle of a story, fully engaged, her hands moving as she talks. Then her attention shifts, just slightly.

She catches her reflection in the window and straightens without breaking conversation—a quick adjustment to her hair, then back to the table as if nothing happened.

It's subtle enough that it doesn't interrupt anything. But it happens again.

None of these moments stand out on their own. They don't feel excessive. They don't feel like a problem. They feel normal.

For a long time, I watched all of this without thinking twice. Because it mirrored something I was doing myself.

Not in obvious ways, but in the same subtle, repetitive patterns that simmer beneath awareness—the second glance in the mirror before leaving the house that turns into a third.

The quick glance at a reflection that lingers a little too long, or the way you suddenly become aware of yourself the moment you feel seen.

It doesn't pull you out of the moment completely, but it changes how you're in it.

I witnessed this so many times during the years I owned a bridal store with my daughter. We opened it shortly after she got married, when we were still riding the high of the wedding—the romance of it, the energy, the way everything felt so magical.

It wasn't about the flowers or the cake or even the dress itself. It was more about the feeling of possibilities and what it all represented.

We imagined what it would feel like to create that experience for other women—to welcome brides and their entourages—the people who loved them most.

Mothers.
Sisters.
Grandmothers.
Bridesmaids.

Everyone gathered as the bride-to-be stepped out of the dressing room and onto the pedestal, turning slowly in front of the mirror... trying to feel it—that fairytale moment—seeing herself walking down the aisle, wondering if this was the dress she would say yes to.

And for many of them, it was exactly that.
But for just as many, something else happened.

They would come out from behind the curtain glowing—excited, hopeful—having just whispered to the consultant, I think this is the one. Then they would step up onto the platform and wait.

For the reaction.
For the confirmation.
For the gasp—the "Oooooh!"
For someone to meet them in that moment and reflect back what they were hoping to feel.

You could feel it in the room—that awkward pause.

And the way her eyes moved quickly from one face to another, searching for it.

She held herself there—almost suspended—waiting for the reaction to land.

Because it wasn't just about the dress. It was about what she was hoping to see in herself... and how she wanted them to see her. To confirm what she felt.

And sometimes, it came. The room lit up. And voices overlapped... there were gasps.

And you could watch her light up—her shoulders lift, her face soften, her body settle into something that felt right.

But when it didn't...
It was quieter.
Not harsh.
Not obvious. Just... not there.

It was more of a delayed response. A polite smile, or a comment that didn't quite match the moment.

"Oh, that's nice..."
"Pretty lace..."
And sometimes, it wasn't subtle at all.

"You look fat."
"I wouldn't choose that."
"You look pregnant."

The words would land, and you could feel the shift happen instantly. Because in that moment, she wasn't just hearing opinions about a dress.

She was hearing something about herself. And in that space, everything changed.

And when she didn't get that reaction—when the moment didn't meet her the way she needed—it wasn't the dress that felt rejected. It was her.

It had the power to either lift her into something she could feel and believe—that she was beautiful—or quietly crush it.

And you could see it happen right before your eyes.

There was a shift.
Her posture changed.
Her shoulders pulled in slightly.
Her eyes softened, but not in a good way.
Her head lowered just enough.

The energy left the room. And the excitement faded.

Those were the moments I knew her tears weren't about the dress—they were about feeling like the women surrounding her didn't think she was beautiful.

That's when you see it. Not in the mirror. But in the moment you let someone else's reaction decide what's true.

If This Feels Like You...

If you've ever asked someone, "Does this look okay?"
when what you were really asking was,"Do I look okay?"

If you've ever felt your mood shift because of someone's reaction to how you looked...

If compliments, reassurance, approval, or attraction felt more powerful than you wanted them to...

If you've ever looked at a photo and immediately focused on yourself first...

If you've ever deleted a picture not because the moment was bad, but because you didn't like how you looked in it...

If you've ever felt your confidence rise or fall
based on someone else's opinion, expression, or response...

If you've ever realized how quickly one comment could pull you back into an old insecurity...

If part of you still searches for confirmation before fully believing you are enough on your own...

If you've ever caught yourself wondering:
Why does this affect me so deeply?
Why do I need reassurance to feel settled?
When did other people's reactions become tied to how I see myself?

You are not alone.

Because many of the beliefs women carry about themselves didn't begin as facts.

They began as moments.
Moments that were repeated, reinforced, internalized, and quietly carried forward for years.

Maybe the real shift happens the moment you stop letting someone else's reaction determine what's true about you?

The moment you see it,
you realize how much of your life
was spent looking for reassurance.

CHAPTER 12

Beneath it All

It used to be subtle. Now it's not.

Women in their 40s and 50s are talking about their bodies, their faces, and the changes they're experiencing in a way that feels more open, more direct, and more unapologetic than ever before.

And they're not just talking about it—they're doing something about it.

Listen to conversations between women in this stage of life and it's not subtle or guarded. It's direct, detailed, and often said with humor.

But underneath it is something else—awareness.

They talk about memory lapses, sleep changes, weight shifts, skin texture, and facial structure in the same way we once talked about periods or pregnancy—openly, honestly, and without apology.

There is also more access to everything than ever before.

There's more information. More options. And more ways to respond to what we're seeing and feeling in our bodies.

Looking back, I realize how privately it all began—it was almost secret or even taboo in the way I experienced my own body.

I never would have imagined that the girl sitting in her bedroom reading *Are You There God? It's Me, Margaret*—50 years ago—would become someone openly talking about her body like this today.

At first, the changes were subtle enough that I questioned them.

The skin on my neck started to look different in pictures—looser somehow, like it belonged to someone older than the person I still felt like inside. My waistline shifted slightly.

There was a new bulge around the back of my bra line that hadn't been there before—nothing dramatic, just enough to make me wonder if I was imagining it.

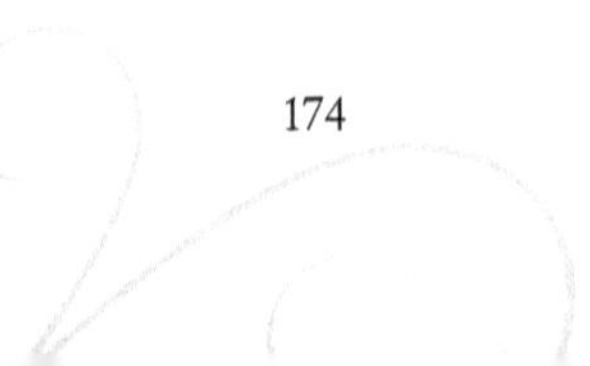

But after months of the same diet and the same fitness routine, and putting in the same effort, there was a moment when it became clear.

I didn't change anything. My body did.

And this wasn't temporary. It was a shift—a new baseline, a new normal.

Now my body wasn't going to respond the way it used to. I tried all the adjustments. And that realization changes how you see everything.

It's no longer about tweaking one thing or correcting it back to what it was.

So I explored—I tried body toning treatments on my stubborn thighs and added laser and RF treatments for my face. I wasn't trying to become a new person. Just fix what the treatments promised.

There's a namc for what's happening now for women in this stage of life—the "meno makeover."

Not a single decision, but a series of small, ongoing adjustments—made over time, as bodies change, with more access, more information, and more options than ever before.

And this isn't new. We're just more focused on fixing it.

Listening to Pirie Jones Grossman talk about her experience, it makes sense. Like many women, she didn't feel pretty growing up.

Now in her 60s, an executive coach who works with women around identity, confidence, and self-worth, she remembers watching it instead—how much it mattered, how much time it took, and how everything had to be just right before a woman could even walk out the door.

Her mother moved through the world that way.

Hair done.
Makeup in place.
Nothing left undone.

She wouldn't even go to the mailbox unless everything was in place. Beauty wasn't something you were. It was something you created.

Even as a child, she could feel what existed underneath it all—the comparison, the constant measuring, and the awareness of where you stood without anyone having to say it out loud.

She was skinny, awkward, and never quite felt pretty in the way other girls seemed to naturally be.

She noticed who got attention and who was admired. And somewhere along the way, she decided she wasn't one of them. That feeling stayed with her longer than she realized.

But there was one memory from childhood that always stood apart from the rest.

Every night, she sat with her father and he would brush her long, dark hair before bed—a small ritual that became so meaningful to her. It was something that belonged just to the two of them. Then one day, her mother took her to the salon.

She sat in the chair watching her hair fall to the floor while her mother stood behind her, instructing the stylist to keep cutting.

She was crying. Begging him to stop. But her mother told him to keep going.

Her hair was gone when he was done—a new pixie cut.

After that, she slowly started learning that if she didn't feel pretty, she would have to find other ways to belong, be valued, or feel seen.

She learned how to speak clearly, think critically, and hold her own. She started writing and joined the debate team.

But something didn't quite line up—she could show up confidently, but didn't completely feel at home in how she looked doing it.

Over time, she adapted. If she couldn't be the pretty one, she would be the likable one. The easy one. The one people enjoyed being around.

And it didn't feel like a strategy. It felt like relief.

When she was 19, a friend convinced her to enter a beauty pageant with her. She didn't believe she belonged there at all. Her friend was the beautiful one—everyone knew it. She felt so out of place on that stage.

Then the unimaginable happened. They called her name—First place! She remembers standing there, thinking they had made a mistake.

She won.

And in that same moment, something happened. Everyone came up to her... congratulating her and hugging her.

But her best friend didn't. She didn't even acknowledge her. She didn't say anything. She just left.

They didn't speak for ten years after that. So what stayed with Pirie wasn't the win. It was what it cost.

Looking back, she sees it differently now. Not just the moment—but what was underneath it.

She talked about how you can feel it immediately when a woman walks into a room—not based on how she looks, but on something else entirely.

"A woman who may not be what you would call traditionally beautiful, but her energy is alive. She's grounded, present, at ease in herself—and you feel it."

She went on to describe the opposite—the kind of presence that may look beautiful on the surface but feels entirely different underneath it.

A woman who is objectively beautiful, but her energy feels flat. Disconnected. Like she's trying. And you feel that too."

Because beauty is something deeper. It's essence. And essence isn't how you look. It's how you feel—to yourself, and to everyone around you—and that is beauty.

That's what she wanted women to know.

But what happens after that is where it gets more complicated.

When changing how you look starts to change how you feel…that's when it begins to stick.This isn't just behavioral. It's neurological.

At its core, this is what psychologists describe as reward-based learning—a system the brain uses to reinforce behaviors that reduce discomfort and create relief.

The moment something catches your attention and feels like something that needs to be addressed, your brain doesn't pause. It looks for a way to resolve it. And the second you believe something might improve it, your brain responds—not because anything has changed yet, but because it could. That anticipation is powerful.

Dopamine—the brain's reward chemical—is released not just after a result, but in the expectation of one. The decision, the research, booking the appointment, even imagining the outcome.

So before anything actually changes, your brain is already associating action with relief.

And that's where the loop begins. You notice something. You decide to do something about it. And you feel better.

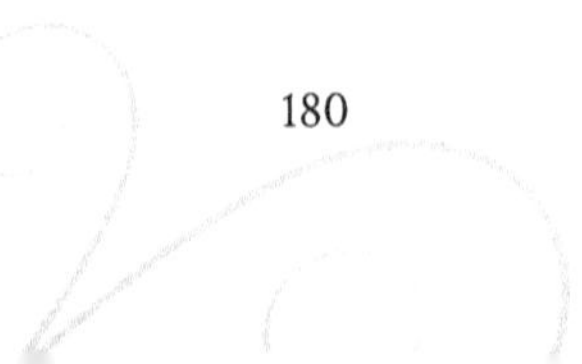

And once that happens a few times, the brain starts to rely on it—not as a conscious choice, but as a learned response.

Yet at the same time, something else begins to shift.

Your perception.

She's in her 50s. She stands in front of the mirror, leaning in slightly, focusing on one small line near her mouth.

It's faint. Just barely noticeable.

But once she sees it, she can't unsee it. It doesn't feel small. It feels obvious—like it's the only thing anyone else sees when they look at her.

Her last Botox appointment was four weeks ago. Her provider told her to come back in twelve weeks. But that doesn't matter.

Because now that she sees it, it feels like something is wrong. Like there's a hole in the boat—and if she doesn't fix it now, it's going to sink. So she starts looking for another provider... another appointment. She needs something sooner so she's figuring out how to get around the wait for her scheduled appointment. Not because anything has actually changed that much, but because it suddenly feels like it has.

That's dysmorphia.

It's seeing a reflection that feels real—but is an exaggerated version of reality.
And once that lens shifts, it's hard to undo. Because once it feels real, it feels urgent.

It's not optional.
And it's not something you can ignore.

And when something feels that way, it feels necessary to respond to.

Which is why stopping the maintenance—doesn't feel easy. It feels like ignoring something. Like you're letting something in that you've spent years trying to keep out.

And that's what keeps people in it. Not necessarily because of vanity or weakness—but because your brain is doing exactly what it was designed to do.

Reinforcing what brings relief. And repeating what feels like control. And over time, the question shifts.

Not: *Do I need to do this?*
But: *How far do I want to take this?*

We may not have stopped to question how it started. But we've learned how to continue it.

If This Feels Like You...

If you've ever looked at yourself and wondered, "How did I get here?"

If you've ever felt surprised that the woman in the mirror didn't completely match the age you still felt inside...

If you've ever caught yourself trying harder to maintain, improve, or hold onto parts of yourself that once felt effortless...

If you've ever noticed how one small flaw could suddenly become impossible to stop focusing on...

If you've ever found yourself doing more and more just to feel like yourself again...

If you've ever wondered: When did maintenance start feeling necessary? Or, when did self-care start feeling like pressure?

How much of this was truly my choice... and how much of it came from the pressure to keep up?

If you've ever questioned whether you were simply making small improvements…
or trying to fight something inevitable…

You are not alone. Because for many women, the struggle isn't really about aging.

It's about identity.

Control.
Relief.
Worth.
And the fear of what it means to let go.

But maybe the real question isn't: "How do I stop this?" Maybe it's: "How much of myself am I willing to lose trying to outrun it?"

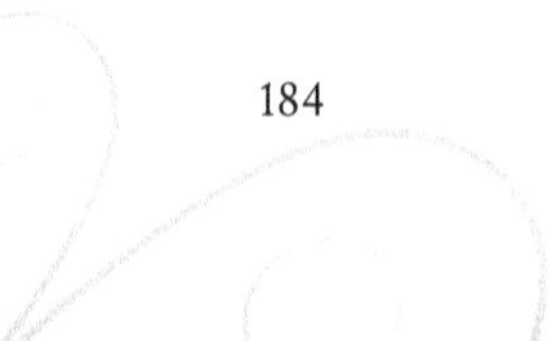

The hardest part isn't seeing it—
it's recognizing that what feels true
isn't always what's real.

What Remains

What Actually Matters
When Everything Else Falls Away

CHAPTER 13

What Actually Lasts

Thinking back to those visits with my Grandma, I understand now what she was trying to show me. Beauty was never just about what the mirror reflects.

It lives far beyond that. And that kind of beauty doesn't fade with time. In fact, in many ways, it grows stronger.

When I was younger, I heard her say it. Beauty is only skin deep. It sounded right. It sounded like something you were supposed to believe. But I didn't get it… it didn't feel true. Not in the world I was growing up in, anyway. Not in the way beauty actually showed up over time.

Because what I saw was something different.

Beauty got attention. It got noticed, and it held value. It shaped how women were seen—and how they saw themselves.

So even though I heard something deeper, I learned something else. I watched it reinforced in subtle ways.

In what was noticed.
In what was praised.
In what seemed to matter most.

But eventually, something begins to shift, and you start noticing different things—not in the mirror, but in people.

You notice the way someone makes you feel when you're around them, the way they listen, the way they speak, and the way they carry themselves without needing to prove anything.

You start to remember people differently, too. Not for their hair, their makeup, or their full lips—but for how they show up. And how they make you feel.

That's what stays with you.

My Grandma didn't move through the world trying to be seen. She didn't change herself to get attention. She stayed true to who she was.

There was something about her that felt grounded. She noticed people. And when something mattered, she said it—quietly, but in a way you felt it. It wasn't for effect.

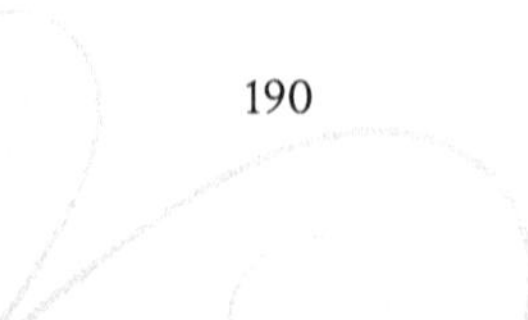

It was because it was genuine.

She didn't need attention—but you noticed her anyway. She was soft-spoken, kind, and incredibly perceptive. The kind of person who understood people without needing many words.

And that stays with you. Long after everything else fades.

There's a question that comes up when you start thinking about what actually lasts.

Not what we hope lasts.
Not what we try to hold onto.

But what really stays. People often say it's the way you made others feel. And for a long time, I understood that concept. But I don't think I fully believed it.

Because how do you really know what stays with someone after a moment has passed? Especially if you never see them again, or lose touch with someone who once meant something to you. How do you know what they carried with them years later? Or whether they knew what you carried too?

Recently, I had an experience that answered that question for me. I reconnected with the woman who took care of my children when they were young. We had lost touch over time, and somehow found our way back to sitting across from each other again at a coffee shop.

Thirty years ago, she was such a big part of our lives. She was like family—right at the heart of our everyday life, in our home and with my children. I trusted her completely. She was everything to us.

She wasn't just helping me—she felt like an extension of me. A second mother to my kids during those years.

And sitting there together more than 30 years later, with our coffee untouched, talking about that time in our lives, she began sharing how deeply those years had impacted her... how loved and valued I had made her feel, and how much our family had meant to her.

And I remember sitting there, taking it all in—feeling humbled, surprised, and honestly a little caught off guard by it. Because in my mind, she was the one who had been of service to us. She was the one who showed up for my family every day with such care and selflessness. And yet—what stayed with her... was how she felt in our home.

Not what I looked like.
Not what I wore. Just how she felt.

And it stayed with her for thirty years.
Just like she did with me.

And that's the part we don't always know. What people carry with them... long after the moment has passed.

For so much of my life, what took up space in my mind was the mirror. How I looked and what needed to be adjusted.

But when I think about what actually stays... It's not that.

It's the moments.
The conversations.
The way a season of life feels while you're in it.
And how you show up inside of it—Not perfectly, or polished. Just present.

Pam, in her early seventies, sees it now. But she didn't always.

In her earlier years, beauty was something she was aware of. Growing up, she was taller than most of the girls around her, and often told she was too skinny. People also told her she was pretty.

It was something she grew up hearing, something she saw reflected in the women around her—

her mother, her sister. It was just... part of the environment.

But right alongside that, there was always something slightly off. Not quite enough... Or almost.

In her marriage, that feeling got louder. She remembers one particular night—it was her birthday. She had bought a new black dress. The kind you put on hoping to be seen.

She walked out, stood in front of him, and asked, "How do I look?"

He barely looked up. "You look fine."

Not harsh. Not cruel. Just... dismissive.
And she remembers what that felt like. Not ugly. Not rejected. Just invisible.

At dinner later that night, she excused herself to the ladies' room and when she came back to the table and noticed something sitting beside her plate. A napkin, folded into a perfect rose.

A stranger had left it for her.
With no conversation.
And no expectation. Just a simple moment of being noticed.

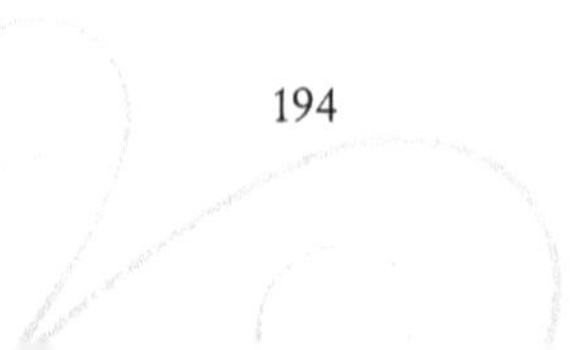

And in that moment, the contrast was undeniable. Not just between two men—but between being acknowledged... and being invisible.

"I just wanted his attention."

After the divorce, attention came easily again. And for a while, it felt validating.

But it didn't just come from men. In her early 40s, it showed up in a unexpected moment—sitting across from a friend.

She reached across the table and touched her forehead. "You don't need much... maybe just a little right here."

It was casual and could have been easy to brush off. But it stuck.

And that's how it starts. Not with dissatisfaction—but with awareness you didn't have five minutes before.

From there, the line starts to move.

A little here.
A little there.
Another adjustment.

And for a moment, it works. "You feel better. And you look better."

Until that becomes the new baseline.

Years later, sitting in her doctor's office before she scheduled a facelift, she told him, "This will be a one and done."

"That's not usually the case," he responded.

And she could see it. Not just in herself, but in others. There was a pattern.

A touch here. A tweak there. There was always something else.

That's where something shifted. Not because my friend stopped caring—she still takes great pride in looking good, feeling put together, and expressing herself through beauty and style. She gets compliments everywhere she goes— about her appearance, her outfits, and the way she gracefully carries herself.

"I've gotten to a place where I feel really good about who I am."

What replaced the chase wasn't indifference. It was something steadier.
Connection.

There's something special about the way she's drawn to people—sometimes without even

knowing why—and when she feels that pull, she speaks it. A compliment. A kind word.

Even if it's something simple, but real. Because she knows how much that can matter. She's felt the impact of a stranger's kind words or gestures.

So now, she gives that to other people. Naturally. Without overthinking it.

Over time, what grounded her wasn't attention anymore. It was something deeper. Her faith.

"I believe God's light in me is part of why people are drawn to me... and without that, I wouldn't feel like a pretty person."

She realized the confidence she chased for years was never going to come from the outside. It came from knowing who she is.

And from that place, everything looks different. The mirror matters less, and the moments more—time with her grandchildren, taking care of her health so she can keep showing up for her life, traveling, and actually being present for a life she loves.

"If you keep chasing how you look, it will never be enough. Because you'll never really get there—it just keeps moving."

Listening to her, I started to hear something familiar—exactly what my grandmother had always said.

Beauty is only skin deep.

But I hear it differently now. Not because what I saw in the mirror was never real—but because it was never the whole story.

If this sounds like you

Have you ever spent more time focused on appearance than the qualities that actually make someone memorable?

Have you ever felt pressure to keep improving how you look while giving far less attention to how you feel, who you are, or what's beneath the surface?

Have you ever thought about stepping away from some of the beauty routines, maintenance, or treatments you've grown used to... but found it harder than you expected?

Have you ever noticed that the people you admire most are often remembered for the way they make others feel?

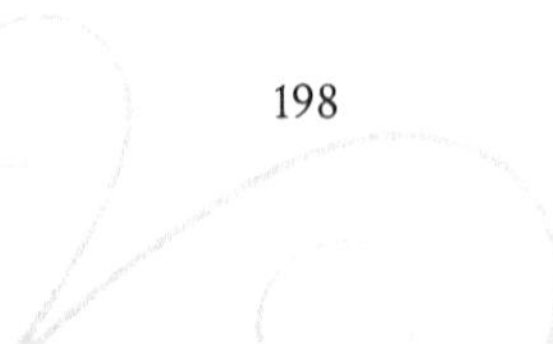

Have you ever wondered:
What do people actually notice about me?
What do they remember after I leave the room?
What part of me truly stays with them?

Have you ever noticed that what leaves the deepest impression on you is rarely someone's appearance?

And if that's true for the people who stay with you... is it also true about you?

Because maybe the real question is not:
"How do I keep time from changing me?"

Maybe it's:
"What part of me matters most in the end?"

What stays isn't what
you saw in the mirror.
It's the life you were actually living.

Final Perspective

What Really Matters

This book is not a judgment. It's an invitation to pause and ask yourself deeper questions about your identity, worth, beauty, and aging... and what all of it really means to you.

The seed for this book was planted awhile ago when I stopped doing Botox after twenty years of routine treatments.

At first, the decision was partly health related. Because I was beginning to experience some of the side effects from it. That led me to start reading more about the effects of long-term use on facial muscles, including weakening over time.

I also became interested in the growing discussion about how limiting facial expression may affect the way we process and express emotion. But underneath that, something else was happening too.

I started questioning myself. How did I get here? At what point had this become part of who I was? Why did this matter so much to me now? And what was my end game?

At the same time, I saw other women trying harder to erase more signs of time.

Getting facelifts as early as 40—continuing to chase a younger version of themselves, and sometimes looking less and less like the person they once were.

I remember thinking to myself:

I don't want that.

And then I noticed something else. Women in their twenties were already starting Botox and fillers before the first wrinkle appeared—not because they were trying to look younger, but because they wanted to look different... more refined, more perfected, more like someone else.

That made me pause.

Not because I think any of it is wrong. Not because I think women shouldn't do whatever makes them feel good about themselves.

But because I realized this conversation mattered.

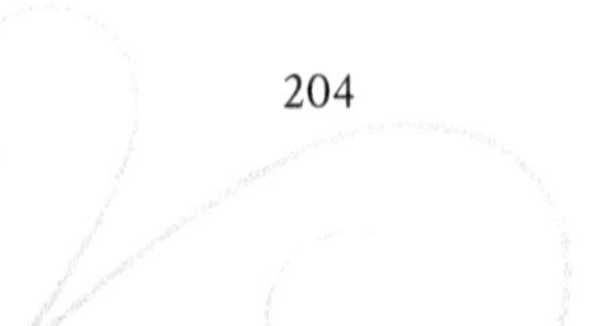

After growing up with self-worth issues, comparison, validation seeking, and years of tying confidence to appearance—and spending decades inside the world of ongoing maintenance myself—I started seeing something more clearly.

The importance placed on physical appearance in our culture seemed to be growing louder while the importance of what was happening within us was growing quieter.

What once felt like nurturing the mind, body, and spirit had gradually become more centered around appearance.

There was a time when we slowly settled into ourselves as we aged. As your appearance changed you had no choice but to accept it. But now that we have the ability to continuously alter ourselves, acceptance becomes more complicated because it's optional.

What can feel empowering can also become a repeated ongoing rejection of ourselves.

And at what cost? Because even if treatments create a temporary sense of confidence or improvement, it's worth asking whether the repeated cycle of finding flaws, correcting them, and briefly feeling better is reinforcing the belief that we were never enough to begin with.

Maybe the real question is: What am I actually searching for underneath all of this?

The more I thought about it, the more I realized this wasn't only about beauty. It was about the way so many of us search for happiness externally.

The perfect partner.
The perfect house.
The perfect outfit.
The ideal weight.
The sculpted cheekbones.
The smooth forehead.
The full lips.

We all have our list. Just hoping the next thing might finally bring contentment, confidence, happiness, or enoughness.

I remember reading about a global study on finding happiness that really stayed with me. The article pointed out that in several other countries, when people wanted to feel happier, they often did something meaningful for someone else.

They volunteered, spent time with family, they reached out, connected or contributed to someone else's happiness in some way.

But, in the United States, people were more likely to do something for themselves. Treat themselves to a spa day, go shopping, dinner out, or beauty treatments.

Neither is inherently wrong.

But it made me think about how much of our culture revolves around trying to feel internally fulfilled through external experiences.

And maybe that's part of what this book is really exploring. Not beauty itself. But what beauty has come to represent.

Things like control, Worth. Visibility. Relevance. Youth. Validation. Safety. Belonging.
And underneath all of that... is fear.

Fear of aging.
Fear of becoming invisible.
Fear of no longer being chosen, admired, desired, or valued.
Fear of irrelevance.
Fear of loneliness.
Fear of death.

Or maybe simply grief for the younger version of ourselves we once recognized in the mirror.

These are not judgments. They are simple questions. And questions worth asking ourselves honestly.

Because maybe the real question is not:
"How do I keep time from changing me?"

Maybe, when it's all said and done, it's more like:
"What part of me matters most in the end?"

www.ingramcontent.com/pod-product-compliance
Lightning Source LLC
LaVergne TN
LVHW010656110826
845149LV00014B/3118

* 9 7 9 8 9 9 3 8 3 2 6 7 8 *